Deliciously Nutritious Heart-Friendly Cookbook

Joey .R Gentry

All rights reserved. Copyright © 2023 Joey .R Gentry

Funny helpful tips:

Stay informed about telemedicine; it's bridging distances and making healthcare more accessible.

Life's puzzle is intricate; each piece, no matter how small, completes the picture.

Deliciously Nutritious Heart-Friendly Cookbook : Heart-Healthy Recipes for a Nutrient-Rich Diet: Tasty and Nourishing Meals to Keep Your Heart Happy and Healthy

<u>Life advices:</u>

Stay loyal; it's the bedrock of a secure relationship.

Stay informed about the potential of liquid biopsies; they promise non-invasive disease detection.

Introduction

Welcome to this book, your comprehensive resource for embracing a healthy and balanced lifestyle. In this guide, we will explore delicious recipes, practical tips, and valuable information to help you achieve your goals of weight loss, lower cholesterol levels, and overall well-being.

We begin our journey with "Delicious Cycle 1 Recipes for Your Rapid Weight Loss," providing you with mouthwatering recipes that are not only satisfying but also designed to support your weight loss efforts. You'll discover a variety of flavorful dishes that will keep you motivated and energized on your journey towards a healthier you.

Next, we delve into the topic of lowering cholesterol levels through diet. Our "Cholesterol Lowering Diet" section provides you with valuable insights into managing your cholesterol levels by making smart food choices. Learn about the importance of a balanced diet, discover cholesterol-lowering foods, and explore recipes that are both heart-healthy and delicious.

In the "Low Carb Diet" section, we explore the benefits of reducing your carbohydrate intake. Discover how a low-carb diet can help you manage your weight, improve your blood sugar control, and enhance overall health. We provide you with practical tips and delicious recipes that will make embracing a low-carb lifestyle enjoyable and sustainable.

To kickstart your day with energy and vitality, we present a variety of breakfast recipes in "Rise and Shine with a Fortified Breakfast." These recipes are designed to provide you with essential nutrients and keep you feeling satisfied throughout the morning.

For a satisfying and nutritious lunch, our "Lunchtime Recipes for Afternoon Energy" section offers a range of flavorful options that will keep you fueled and focused throughout the day. From refreshing salads to hearty soups, you'll find plenty of inspiration to make your lunchtime meals both enjoyable and nourishing.

In "Great Dinner Surprises," we present a collection of dinner recipes that are not only delicious but also promote a low-carb and low-cholesterol lifestyle. Explore creative and flavorful dishes that will make dinnertime a highlight of your day.

Complement your main meals with our "Unique Side Dishes" section, where you'll find innovative and healthy recipes to add variety and balance to your plate. These side dishes are packed with flavor and nutrients, making them the perfect accompaniment to any meal.

In "Fulfillment with Drinks," we offer refreshing beverage ideas that are low in carbs and cholesterol-friendly. From smoothies and infused waters to herbal teas, these drinks will quench your thirst while providing you with nourishment and hydration.

Snacking doesn't have to derail your goals. Our "Make Ahead Snacks" section provides you with convenient and nutritious snack options that you can prepare in advance. These snacks will keep you satisfied between meals and help you maintain a low-carb and low-cholesterol lifestyle.

When the weather calls for outdoor dining, "Let's Have a Picnic" offers ideas and recipes for a delightful and healthy picnic experience. Discover portable and delicious dishes that are perfect for enjoying nature while staying true to your dietary goals.

We understand the importance of satisfying your sweet tooth without compromising your health. In "Exciting Desserts," we present low-carb and low-cholesterol dessert recipes that will indulge your cravings while keeping you on track with your wellness journey.

In addition to the low-carb and low-cholesterol focus, we expand our culinary exploration with the "Paleolithic Cookbook" section. Learn about the paleo lifestyle, its benefits, and how to incorporate it into your daily routine. Explore a sample meal plan and discover delicious paleo recipes that embrace natural and whole foods.

We conclude our guide with the "Baby Food Diet" section, which introduces you to a unique approach to weight loss. Discover the principles of the baby food diet and how it can help you achieve your weight loss goals in a nutritious and sustainable way.

Throughout this guide, we provide tips for prepping, guidance for incorporating these dietary approaches into your day-to-day life, and valuable insights to support your overall wellness journey.

Embrace the power of low-carb and low-cholesterol living as you embark on a path towards better health and vitality. Let this guide be your companion as you explore a wide range of delicious recipes, practical tips, and informative content that will empower you to make positive choices and create a sustainable and fulfilling lifestyle.

Contents

17 Day Diet Cookbook Reloaded: Delicious Cycle 1 Recipes Cookbook For Your Rapid Weight Loss 1

Cholesterol Lowering Diet 76

Introduction 77

Section 1: Low Carb Diet...80

Chapter 1: Rise and Shine with a Fortified Breakfast 82

Chapter 2: Lunchtime Recipes for Afternoon Energy...94

Chapter 3: Great Dinner Surprises 105

Chapter 4: Unique Side Dishes...114

Chapter 5: Fulfillment with Drinks 119

Chapter 6: Make Ahead Snacks 126

Chapter 7: Let's Have a Picnic..136

Chapter 8: Exciting Desserts...143

Chapter 9: Wise Wok Cooking..153

Chapter 11: Tips for Prepping 169

Section 2: Paleolithic Cookbook 174

What is Paleo? 175

Why Go the Paleolithic Route? 176

Benefits of the Paleo Lifestyle 176

Paleo Food Types..178

Paleo Confusion 179

Sample Daily Meal Plan for Beginners 183

Eating Paleo in Day to Day Life 184

Recipe Ideas...186

- Lunch Recipes 189
- Dinner Recipes 191
- Sides 192
- Roast Vegetables in Orange andRosemary 192
- Meats 194
- Poultry 199
- Snacks 205
- Paleolithic Cookbook Conclusion 210
- Baby Food Diet 211
- Achieve Weight Loss With The Baby Food Diet 211

17 Day Diet Cookbook Reloaded:
Delicious Cycle 1 Recipes Cookbook For Your Rapid Weight Loss

Introduction

The 17 Day Diet is made up four Cycles which aim to promote fast and healthy weight loss through these four core ideas:

- Accelerate,

- Activate,

- Achieve, and

- Arrive.

Each Cycle lasts for 17 days, during which a person is given a list of approved foods that he or she must strictly adhere to for the success of the program. The secret of this program lies on what is known as body confusion that is achieved through the changing food patterns throughout the four Cycles. This body confusion is a way of preventing the body from adapting to the metabolic properties that allow you to burn more fat faster.

Cycle 1 is the initial 17-day period that will keep you away from all the starchy foods, sugars, and carbohydrates that you know and love. It is considered to be the strictest of all the cycles, but also allows the most weight loss as it cleanses the body of unhealthy carbs that result to all those extra pounds. Furthermore, this cycle stimulates the body's metabolic rate, allowing it to burn up fat and calories faster.

The good thing about this first cycle is that while you may be deprived of all the pasta, breads, and sweets that you have grown to want and love, it does

allow you to eat unlimited amounts of certain proteins and vegetables, keeping you from depriving your body of the nutrients that it needs. Here is

a list of some of the most delicious recipes that you can try out during your

Cycle 1 period.

Breakfast Recipes

Breakfast Bowl

This breakfast treat is easy to do and very filling. Most of the ingredients are already those that you may have on hand, so it is not easy to prepare either.

Ingredients:

- ¼ cup Ground Turkey
- ¼ cup Mushrooms
- ¼ cup Bell Peppers (sliced and frozen)
- ¼ cup Roasted Bell Peppers
- 2 pcs. Egg whites
- ¼ cup Mozzarella, shredded

Procedure:

1. Prepare all the ingredients and keep the handy and ready to use.
2. In a medium-sized pan, heat about 1 tablespoon of vegetable oil.
3. Sautee the mushrooms and bell-peppers, and add in the turkey sausage.
4. When the meat is tender, add the egg whites and stir until cooked.
5. Season with salt and pepper to your preferred taste.

6. Transfer to a plate, sprinkle with shredded mozzarella cheese.

7. Enjoy!

You can also change or add vegetables such as substituting tomatoes for the bell-peppers and adding onions to the recipe. The good thing about this recipe is you can practically use whatever vegetable you have and come up with a healthy egg-white omelette that will give you the energy to start your day.

Mock French Toast

French toast has always been a breakfast favourite for many people, and with this recipe, you can have it and still stick to your diet as well. For this breakfast treat, all you need are 2 simple ingredients and some flavouring for taste. This recipe is also sometimes referred to as apple pancakes.

Ingredients:

- 1 Apple

- 1 pc Whole Egg or 2pcs Egg whites

- *cinnamon or vanilla to taste

Procedure:

1. Spray some oil onto a skillet or put just enough oil to coat the bottom of the pan, and then turn the heat on to medium.

2. Slice the apples into thin pieces. Make sure to remove the core or the seeds.

3. When the pan is hot, lay the apples on the bottom of the pan so that no apples are overlapping.

4. Cover the pan, lower the heat, and cook for about 2minutes or until the apple slices are softened.

5. Meanwhile, whisk your egg or egg whites and add about a teaspoon of cinnamon and 1/4teaspoon vanilla. Mix well.

6. Pour the egg mixture over the apples and let all the egg cook. Try to lift the parts that are already cooked to let the raw egg flow to the bottom of the pan to be cooked.

7. When there is no more liquid egg left, cover the pan and cook for another 2minutes.

8. Flip the eggs onto the other side. Cover and cook again for another minute or so.

9. Slide onto your plate. Enjoy!

For an added treat, top off with fat-free yogurt. Truly yummy and satisfying!

Baked Apple Tarts

This is very similar to the Mock French Toast, with the only difference being in the cooking method used. If you have more time on your hands or if you would rather just leave the cooking to your oven, this recipe should be just right for you.

Ingredients:

- 1 pc Apple, cored and thinly sliced
- 1 pc Egg or 2 pcs Egg whites
- 1 teaspoon Cinnamon
- ¼ teaspoon Vanilla

Procedure:

1. Pre-heat your oven to 375°F.
2. In a baking pan, line the thin slices of apple so that they cover the bottom of the pan.
3. Whish the eggs with the cinnamon and vanilla, and pour over the apples.
4. Bake for about five minutes or until the apples are soft and the egg is cooked through.
5. Serve and enjoy.

You can also use a microwave-safe dish and cook this in the microwave for about 2-3minutes. This is a good way to satisfy your sweet tooth too.

Favorite Breakfast

This recipe is fairly easy to do, and can easily be done ahead of time for that quick and satisfying breakfast. It is really filling as well and packs a lot of vegetables for a really healthy dish.

Ingredients:

- 5 cups Fresh Baby Spinach
- 6 large pcs Mushrooms
- 4 large pcs Tomatoes
- 1/3 cup Onions, chopped
- 2-3 cloves Garlic, minced
- White wine vinegar or Balsamic vinegar
- Salt and Pepper to taste
- 2 Tablespoons Olive Oil

Procedure:

1. Prepare your ingredients. Slice the mushrooms, tomatoes, and onions. Mince the garlic and chop the fresh baby spinach. Prepare a bow to fit all ingredients later.

2. Heat some of the olive oil in a pan, then sauté the mushrooms and set aside in the bowl.

3. Next, sauté the onions, add the garlic, and sauté the tomatoes as well.

Set aside with the mushrooms.

4. Pour in all of the remaining olive oil onto the pan and sauté the baby spinach until cooked.

5. Carefully stir in all the other ingredients back into the pan with the baby spinach.

6. Add a splash of vinegar, about 1 tablespoon or so.

7. Sprinkle with salt and pepper to taste.

8. Transfer to plate and serve.

For a more filling meal, get a portion of the vegetables and mix with scrambled eggs. Also makes a great snack! You can store in an airtight container and keep in the freezer until ready to cook.

Feta and Spinach Egg Omelette

You can never have enough eggs when you're in cycle 1. The good thing is, eggs are so versatile that you can cook them up with almost anything you want so that you never get tired of it. Here is a simple scrambled egg recipe that uses feta cheese for that slightly salty and tangy flavour.

Ingredients:

- 1 Egg or 2pcs Egg whites
- 1 cup Spinach, chopped
- ¼ cup Feta cheese, grated

Procedure:

1. Spray a cooking pan with some oil, or pour a little amount just enough to grease the bottom of the pan.
2. Whish the eggs, add the chopped spinach and the grated feta cheese.
3. Pour egg mixture onto pan and cook at medium heat until there is no more liquid egg left.
4. Serve onto plate. Enjoy!

You can also add some cooked Tempeh bacon for additional flavour. Tempeh is an approved probiotic for cycle 1 that can be bought in most whole foods and vegetarian stores.

Greek Eggs Level Up

Greek eggs are typically scrambled eggs with feta cheese. Because of the salty taste of the cheese, there is no need to add any additional seasoning. Here is a recipe that adds a bit more kick to the classic dish, and it will definitely help you put a fresh start to your day.

Ingredients:

- 2 Whole Eggs or 4pcs Egg whites
- 2 Tablespoons Feta Cheese, fat-free
- ¼ cup Tomatoes
- ¼ cup Bell peppers
- 1/8 tsp. Salt
- Green Onions
- Cumin
- Lemon Juice

Procedure:

1. Cut up the tomatoes, bell peppers and green onions.
2. Scramble the eggs. Mix in the vegetables.
3. Tear up the feta cheese into pieces and mix into the egg mixture.
4. Season with a pinch or two of cumin, depending if you like it hot, then add a splash of lemon juice.
5. Spray a pan with some oil, just until the bottom is greased, then put

over medium heat.

6. When the pan is hot, pour in the scrambled egg and cook until preferred doneness. Make sure that there is no more liquid in the eggs.

7. Serve on a plate and enjoy!

You can adjust the seasoning depending on your taste. Either add more cumin or extra spices, or just remove them altogether. By doing so, you can

enjoy this dish but make it a different taste every time.

Mushroom, Cheese, and Green Pepper Omelette

Just what the name says: an omelette filled with mushrooms, cheese, and

green peppers. A perfect way to start your day!

Ingredients:

- ½ cup Mushrooms, chopped

- ½ Onion, minced

- 1 oz. Fat-free Cheddar Cheese, thinly sliced

- ¼ Green Bell pepper, chopped

- 2 Eggs

- 1 tablespoon Olive Oil

- *Salt and Pepper to taste

Procedure:

1. Pour olive oil in a skillet over medium heat.

2. Sauté the onions, add the mushrooms, and then the green pepper.

3. Meanwhile, whisk the eggs and season with salt and pepper.

4. Add the cheese slices onto the skillet and then pour the egg over all the other ingredients.

5. Fry the omelette for about two minutes before flipping over to cook the other side.

6. Serve on a plate and enjoy!

Make sure that the egg is cooked all the way through and don't worry if it breaks when you try to flip it. This recipe is still guaranteed to taste great!

Main Entrees

Chicken Breast

This dish is very easy to do, straightforward, and still makes up a satisfying meal. The ingredients are also what you would have on hand so preparing it would be a breeze.

Ingredients:

- Chicken Breast
- 1 whole Onion, chopped
- 1 tablespoon Olive Oil
- ½ cup Water
- Salt and Pepper to taste

Procedure:

1. Season the chicken breast with salt and pepper.

2. Prepare a grilling pan over medium heat, put 1 tablespoon of olive oil.

3. When the pan is hot, put the chicken in, add the chopped onions, and pour half a cup of water over the chicken.

4. Cook for about 20minutes or until the chicken is tender and cooked through.

5. Serve.

You can also bake this in a 400°F oven for thirty minutes or until golden brown in color. Yummy and healthy!

Balsamic Chicken Breasts

Here is a dish that makes use of a simple but flavourful marinade which can be made in just a few minutes. Perfect for chicken breasts, the marinade can also be used for other white meats such as fish.

Ingredients:

- ½ cup Balsamic Vinegar
- 1 tablespoon Olive oil
- 1 tablespoon Rosemary, chopped
- 1 clove Garlic, minced
- ½ teaspoon Salt
- ¼ teaspoon Pepper
- 4 pcs Boneless Chicken Breasts, skin removed

Procedure:

1. Create marinade. Combine vinegar, olive oil, rosemary, garlic, salt and pepper in a bowl.

2. Soak chicken breasts into marinade. Marinate for at least 30minutes.

3. Grill chicken breasts for about 8minutes on each side or bake at 350°F for 20-30minutes or until completely cooked through.

4. Transfer onto plate and enjoy!

You can also prepare this dish ahead of time and leave the chicken in the marinade overnight for a stronger flavour.

Balsamic Mustard Chicken Breast

Here is another easy marinade for a tasty chicken breast recipe! If you think that chicken breasts are bland and dry, try this recipe with balsamic vinegar and mustard and you may just change your mind.

Ingredients:

- 3 tablespoons Balsamic Vinegar

- 2 tablespoons Dijon Mustard

- ½ teaspoon Garlic, minced

- 1pc. Chicken Breast

Procedure:

1. Combine the vinegar, mustard, and minced garlic to create the marinade.

2. Coat the chicken in the marinade for at least 30 minutes. The longer you marinate the chicken, the better.

3. When ready to cook, heat a non-stick pan on medium heat. Place the chicken on the pan and pour the remaining marinade over the chicken.

4. Cook on each side for about 5 minutes or until slightly browned.

5. Serve on plate and enjoy!

You can adjust the ingredients according to your preferred taste. If the marinade dries out during cooking, you can add a little more vinegar to avoid the chicken from becoming dry. You can also add some sliced onions and mushrooms for added taste and texture. Also, try to make this ahead of time to let the chicken soak in the marinade longer.

Parmesan Chicken

A simple chicken recipe added with a cheesy twist! This is a great way to serve chicken in a different style.

Ingredients:

- 1lb. Chicken Breast
- 2 Eggs or 4 Egg Whites
- 4 tablespoons Water
- 2 tablespoons Olive Oil
- ¼-1/2 cup Parmesan Cheese, fat-free
- 1 teaspoon Garlic Powder
- *Salt and Pepper to taste

Procedure:

1. Mix the dry ingredients: parmesan cheese, garlic powder, and salt and pepper in a bowl or zip lock bag.
2. Cut the chicken into strips or chunks, whichever you prefer.
3. Beat the eggs with the water.
4. Dip the chicken pieces in the egg before putting in the seasoning bag or bowl.
5. Shake the chicken to coat all pieces with the seasoning.
6. In a pan over medium heat, put the olive oil.
7. Cook the chicken in the pan until golden brown.

8. Transfer to plate. Enjoy!

Make sure to use fat-free parmesan cheese. You can also bake this dish at 350°F for a healthier alternative.

Chicken Stir Fry

Stir fries are great meals to make. They are complete with meat and vegetables, easy to cook, and very tasty and flavourful. Here is a simple stir fry recipe that is perfect for your Cycle 1 diet.

Ingredients:

- ½ cup Broccoli, chopped

- 1pc. Carrot, cut into strips

- 1 whole Onion, chopped

- 1pc. Chicken Breast
- *Salt and Pepper to taste

Procedure:

1. Prepare the ingredients. Chop the broccoli, cut the carrots into thin strips, chop the onion, and cut the chicken breast into strips or cubes.

2. Heat a non-stick pan over medium heat. When the pan is hot enough, toss in the onions and add the carrots and the broccoli. Cook until the carrots are a bit tender. Set aside in a bowl.

3. Put the chicken into the pan. Cover and let cook for about 10minutes, stirring occasionally to make sure that the chicken is cooked all the way through.

4. When the chicken is cooked, mix the vegetables back into the pan, sprinkle with salt and pepper to taste, and cook for another minute or two.

5. Serve on a plate and enjoy.

For added flavour, you can add a splash of light soy sauce into your stir fry while the vegetables and chicken are cooking. Make sure to let the chicken and vegetables absorb the liquid for a more flavourful chicken stir fry. You can also add mushrooms and other vegetables that you may have on hand.

Chicken with Mushrooms and Onions

This is a simple marinated chicken that is topped off with mushrooms and onions. Very simple to make but is a great dish even for those who are not on a diet.

Ingredients:

- 2pcs. Chicken Breasts
- 1 teaspoon Olive Oil
- 1 Lemon, juiced
- 2 cloves Garlic, minced
- ½ teaspoon Black Pepper
- ½ cup Water
- 1pc Onion, chopped
- ½ cup Mushrooms
- 2 tablespoons Light Soy Sauce

Procedure:

1. Combine the olive oil, lemon juice, minced garlic, and black pepper in a zip lock bag.

2. Cut the chicken into strips or chunks. Put into the zip lock bag and marinate for 30minutes or more.

3. When ready to cook, heat a non-stick pan over medium heat and toss

in the chicken and all of the marinade into the pan. Cook for 8-10minutes, stirring occasionally. When the chicken pieces are cooked

all the way through, transfer to a plate and cover to keep it from cooling. Do not turn off the heat.

4. Pour half a cup of water into the pan, and then toss in the onions and

the mushroom. Sautee until the onion becomes soft and the

mushrooms release their moisture.

5. Season with salt and pepper, and then add the 2 tablespoons of light

soy sauce.

6. Top the chicken with the mushrooms and onions. Enjoy!

Devilled Chicken

Chicken is a very versatile meat and can fit with almost any seasoning to satisfy all palates. If you like your chicken a bit on the spicy side, then this recipe is just for you.

Ingredients:

- 4pcs Chicken Breasts
- 1 tablespoon Olive Oil
- 1 tablespoon Apple Cider Vinegar
- 1 tablespoon Yellow Mustard
- ½ teaspoon Cayenne Pepper

Procedure:

1. Mix the olive oil, apple cider vinegar, yellow mustard and cayenne pepper in a bowl.

2. Rub the mixture onto the chicken breasts and marinate for at least 30minutes.

3. Pre-heat the oven to 375°F.

4. When the chicken has been marinated and the oven is at the desired temperature, bake the chicken for 40 minutes or until the chicken is tender.

5. Transfer to a plate and enjoy.

If you want to adjust the spice, simply modify the amount of cayenne pepper in the recipe. You can also grill the chicken and brush with the marinade while doing so to keep the chicken from being too dry.

Greek Chicken Patties

Chicken patties can taste as good as if not better than the regular beef patties that many people are used to. With the addition of some feta cheese,

roasted tomatoes, and some fresh baby spinach, this dish will make you re-

think what a burger patty should be like.

Ingredients:

- 1 kilo Ground Chicken

- 1 pack, Fresh Baby Spinach

- ½ cup Roasted Tomatoes, chopped

- 3 cloves Garlic, crushed

- ½ cup Red Onion, chopped

- ¼-½ cup Fat-free Feta Cheese

- Pepper to taste

Procedure:

1. In a non-stick pan, sauté baby spinach until soft. Set aside and chop

into small pieces.

2. Sauté the onion and garlic, then add to the baby spinach.

3. Add the chopped roasted tomatoes, and then add the ground chicken when the spinach and onion and garlic have cooled down. Sprinkle some pepper to taste.

4. When the chicken has been combined well with the other ingredients, mix in the chopped feta cheese.

5. Create small patties by rounding even potions into a ball and flattening the meat.

6. Cook the patties on the non-stick pan for about 3minutes on each side, or until the patty has cooked through.

7. Serve on a plate and enjoy!

You can store the patties in the freezer for future use. This is also great with a serving of fresh salad on the side. Yummy!

Grilled Balsamic Chicken

Here is another chicken marinade that is sure to be a favourite. Balsamic vinegar and mustards are used to create a slightly tangy, spicy flavour, while the Worcestershire sauce balances it all out to make a delectable dish. Prepare this recipe ahead of time to get the best results.

Ingredients:

- 6pcs Boneless Chicken Breasts, halved

- ¼ cup Fat-free Chicken Broth

- ½ cup Balsamic Vinegar

- 1/3 cup Scallion, chopped

- 2 tablespoons Dijon Mustard

- 1 tablespoon Garlic, minced

- 1 tablespoon Truvia Sweetener

- 2 teaspoons Worcestershire Sauce

- 1 teaspoon Dry Mustard

- 1 teaspoon Cracked Black Pepper

Procedure:

1. Combine the chicken broth, balsamic vinegar, chopped scallions, Dijon mustard, minced garlic, Truvia sweetener, Worcestershire sauce, dry mustard, and cracked black pepper in a large zip lock bag. Make sure that the bag is big enough for you to put in the chicken breasts as well.

2. Mix all the ingredients well to create the marinade.

3. Place the chicken in the zip lock bag and seal.

4. Store in the refrigerator and let the chicken marinate overnight. Make sure to turn it over occasionally to make sure that all parts of the chicken breasts are coated nicely.

5. When ready to cook, prepare your grill.

6. Grill the chicken for about 5minutes on each side or until golden brown in color. Make sure to brush with the marinade from time to time so

that the chicken does not dry out.

7. Serve and enjoy!

Lemon Chicken

This is an easy chicken recipe that makes use of chicken broth, a lemon, rosemary, and some pepper. Yup, all the ingredients you need are simple to have, and the dish is even simpler to prepare. There is also no need to marinade the chicken for a long time so this is an excellent dish to make for when you are just tired and hungry from a long day at work.

Ingredients:

- 1 tablespoon Olive Oil
- 2pcs Chicken Breasts, halved
- 1 cup Low Sodium Chicken Broth
- 1pc. Lemon, zested and juiced
- 1 teaspoon Rosemary
- *Ground Pepper to taste

Procedure:

1. Heat the olive oil in a pan over medium heat.

2. Cook the chicken on the pan for about 4minutes on each side or until slightly browned.

3. Meanwhile, mix all the other ingredients in a bowl: Pour in the chicken broth, add the lemon zest and the lemon juice, mix in 1 teaspoon of rosemary and a pinch or two of ground black pepper. Mix well.

4. When the chicken has been browned on both sides, pour the lemon mixture over the chicken and cover the pan. Let the chicken cook for another 30minutes or until the chicken is cooked through.

5. Serve on a plate, enjoy!

You can substitute the rosemary for other herbs such as thyme or basil, whichever you prefer. The best thing about this recipe is that it is easy to do and it also gives you time for other things as well.

Sesame Chicken Stir Fry

Here is another chicken recipe that is easy to prepare and to cook. Stir fries are always a great way to combine simple ingredients and turn them into a meal that is truly satisfying. Did I mention how easy it is to do this recipe?

Ingredients:

- 1 pc. Chicken Breast, cut into chunks
- 1 small Red Bell pepper
- 1 teaspoon Garlic powder
- ¼ cup Mushrooms
- ¼ cup Fresh Green Beans
- ¼ cup Low Sodium Light Soy Sauce
- 2 teaspoons Olive Oil
- 1 tablespoon Sesame Seeds

Procedure:

1. In a pan over medium heat, place the chicken chunks and pour in the light soy sauce and olive oil. Stir occasionally and let cook until the chicken pieces are browned.

2. Chop all the vegetable ingredients and add to the chicken.

3. Sprinkle in the garlic powder and add the sesame seeds, then sauté until the vegetables are lightly cooked.

4. Serve and enjoy.

Oregano Chicken

You can never have too much chicken for your Cycle 1 period. The good thing is that there are a great number of ways on how to cook chicken and not let it taste the same way over and over again. This simple recipe makes use of seasonings that are already available in most homes.

Ingredients:

- 2 pcs. Chicken Breasts, de-boned and with skin removed
- 2 tablespoons Olive Oil
- 2 tablespoons Lemon Juice
- 1 tablespoon Worcestershire Sauce
- 1 tablespoon Low Sodium Soy Sauce
- 1 teaspoon Dried Oregano Leaves
- ½ teaspoon Garlic Powder
- 2 cloves Garlic, minced
- *Salt and Pepper to taste

Procedure:

1. Combine the olive oil, lemon juice, Worcestershire sauce, soy sauce, oregano leaves, garlic powder, and minced garlic in a bowl and mix.

2. Season the chicken with salt and pepper and lay the pieces on an oven proof dish.

3. Pour the olive oil mixture over the chicken, cover, and let it marinate for 30minutes or more. Make sure to turn the chicken pieces occasionally to coat all sides properly.

4. Pre-heat the oven to 375°F.

5. When the oven is heated up, bake the chicken for 15minutes. Turn the chicken pieces onto the other side and bake for another 15minutes or until the chicken is cooked through.

6. Serve the chicken on a plate and pour the remaining sauce over it or into a separate bowl.

7. Enjoy.

Baked Parmesan Chicken

This chicken recipe is a real gourmet treat! You can serve it during parties or for special occasions, and it lets you stick to your diet too.

Ingredients:

- 1 lb. Chicken Breast, cut into strips or chunks

- ½ cup Fat-free Parmesan Cheese

- ½ teaspoon Salt

- ¼ teaspoon Pepper

- ¼ teaspoon Garlic Powder

- ½ tablespoon Basil

- 1 cup Sugar-free Marinara Sauce

- ½ cup Fat-free Mozzarella

Procedure:

1. In a zip lock bag, combine half cup parmesan cheese, salt, pepper, garlic powder, and basil.

2. Mix the chicken chunks or strips into the dry ingredients and shake well to coat all pieces.

3. Pre-heat the oven to 350°F.

4. Transfer the chicken to an oven-proof dish and top with 1cup of sugar-free marinara sauce.

5. Top with half cup of fat-free mozzarella.

6. Cover with foil and bake for 30minutes or until chicken is cooked through.

7. Serve and enjoy!

Twice-cooked Chicken

While this dish may require a little more effort than most recipes, it is sure to be tender, tasty, and an all-time favourite.

Ingredients:

- 1 tablespoon Olive Oil
- 3pcs Chicken Breasts, de-boned and skins removed
- ½ pc. Onion

- 6 pcs. Large Mushrooms

Procedure:

1. Cook the chicken in a non-stick pan over medium heat until lightly browned. Transfer the chicken to an oven-safe dish and set aside.

2. Meanwhile, pre-heat the oven to 325°F, slice the onions and the mushrooms.

3. Sauté the onions and the mushrooms in the pan where the chicken was cooked. This will take about 3-4 minutes

4. Spoon the onions and the mushrooms over the chicken then cover with foil.

5. Bake in the pre-heated oven for 45 minutes or until the chicken is cooked all the way through.

6. Serve onto plates and enjoy!

Stuffed Chicken Breasts

Chicken with a secret surprise inside. A real treat!

Ingredients:

- 4 pcs Chicken Breasts

- 4 oz. Fat-free Cottage Cheese

- 3 tablespoons Spinach, diced

- 1 teaspoon Garlic Powder

- 1 teaspoon Onion Powder

- 1 tablespoon Parmesan Cheese

- 1 teaspoon Black Pepper

Procedure:

1. Pound the chicken breasts and flatten nicely.

2. Mix the cottage cheese, chopped onions, diced spinach, garlic powder, and black pepper.

3. Place about 3spoonfuls of the cheese mixture at the center of two of the chicken breasts, and then cover each with the remaining chicken breasts. You can use toothpicks to hold the chicken pieces together.

4. Pre-heat the oven to 400°F

5. Place the stuffed chicken in an oven-proof dish and bake in the pre-heated oven for 35-40minutes.

6. Enjoy!

Stuffed Turkey Patties

Here is a turkey recipe that will give you a break from all those chicken dishes for your diet program. Turkey patties are stuffed with onion and cheese to keep it flavourful and tasty.

Ingredients:

- 1 lb. Ground Turkey
- 1 Onion, diced

- ½ cup Fat-free Feta Cheese

- 1 teaspoon Olive Oil

Procedure:

1. Dice the onion and cut the fat-free feta cheese into small pieces.

2. Divide the ground turkey into 3 equal portions.

3. Flatten one portion of the ground turkey on the palm of your hand, and then place a spoonful of the cheese and onion mixture on the center. Ball up the turkey meat to cover the cheese and onion, and then lightly flatten to form a patty. Repeat for the remaining turkey and cheese and onion mixture.

4. Heat the olive oil in a pan over medium heat, then cook the patties one at a time. Each side should take about 2-3mins. each.

5. Serve and enjoy!

Sweet and Sour Turkey Stir-fry

You don't always hear of a turkey stir-fry, but why not? This dish is delicious, healthy, and brings a twist to stir-fry dishes.

Ingredients:

- ¼ lb. Lean Ground Turkey

- ½ Onion, minced

- ¼ Red Bell Pepper, diced

- ½ Red Apple, diced

- ½ teaspoon cinnamon

- ½ teaspoon Lemon Juice

- 3 tablespoons Sugar-free Strawberry Jam

- 1 tablespoon Olive Oil

Procedure:

1. Heat 1 tablespoon of olive oil in a pan over medium heat.

2. Sauté the onions, red bell peppers and apple just until the onions are soft and translucent.

3. Add the lean turkey, season with cinnamon and lemon juice, and then add the fat-free strawberry jam.

4. Sauté until the turkey is cooked.

5. Transfer to plate and enjoy.

Turkey Meatballs

Turkey can be just as good as other meats but much healthier. This recipe allows you to enjoy classic favourite, meatballs, and do so with the healthy twist of turkey meat.

Ingredients:

- 1 lb. Ground Turkey
- ½ teaspoon Oregano
- ½ teaspoon Basil

- ½ teaspoon Garlic, minced
- ½ teaspoon Parsley
- 1 Egg
- 3 oz. Tomato Sauce
- ¼ cup Parmesan Cheese
- ¼ cup Green Pepper, diced
- 1 Onion, diced
- 2 tablespoons Olive Oil

Procedure:

1. Place all the ingredients except the olive oil in a bowl and mix it all together to create a uniform mixture.

2. Measure out 1 tablespoon of the mixture and form into a ball. Do with the rest of the mixture.

3. Heat the olive oil in a non-stick pan over medium heat. When the oil is hot, place the turkey meatballs in the pan and cook for about 15minutes, or until the outside is browned and crispy. Make sure that the turkey is cooked all the way through.

4. Serve and enjoy!

Turkey Meatloaf

This recipe is very easy to do but packs very strong flavors. It can be made ahead of time or can be stored in the refrigerator after cooking for future use.

Ingredients:

- 1 lb. Ground Turkey
- 2 tablespoons Worcestershire Sauce
- 1 Onion, diced
- ½ teaspoon Salt
- ¼ teaspoon Garlic Powder
- ½ teaspoon Sage
- ¼ cup Low fat Blue Cheese
- ½ teaspoon Pepper

Procedure:

1. Combine all the ingredients in a bowl and mix together until you have a uniform blend.
2. Shape into a loaf and place on an oven-safe dish.
3. Pre-heat the oven to 350°F.
4. Bake the turkey meatloaf for 1 hour or until the meat is browned and cooked through.

5. Serve and enjoy.

Baked Tilapia

Many people like to cook tilapia because it is quite easy to prepare and it is known for absorbing flavours very well. One healthy way to serve it is by baking it in the oven.

Ingredients:

- 4 pcs. tilapia fillets, measuring approximately 1.5 lbs. in total

- 2 tbsp. lemon juice (around 30 mL)

- 1 tbsp. virgin olive oil

- 2 tsp. oregano

- ½ tsp. paprika

- 1 tbsp. freshly chopped parsley

- Salt and pepper to taste

- ¼ cup Parmesan cheese, grated (optional)

Procedure:

1. Pre-heat your oven to 400°F.

2. Prepare a flat baking sheet and cover it with parchment paper. You could apply non-stick cooking spray on the baking sheet or you could use aluminum foil if you don't have any parchment paper at home. Make sure the aluminum foil is of high quality so that the lemon juice will not react with it.

3. Rinse and clean the tilapia fillets in cool, running water. When you're done, dry the fillets by patting them using clean paper towels.

4. Using a small bowl, mix the virgin olive oil and the lemon juice. Stir well. If you prefer a stronger lemon taste, you may choose to add up to 2 more tbsps. of lemon juice to this recipe.

5. Add the oregano, paprika, parsley, salt, and pepper to your lemon and virgin oil mixture.

6. Put the fillets on the baking sheet, making sure that they are evenly spaced apart.

7. Pour the combined lemon mixture over the fillets. Use a brush to make sure that the mixture is well-absorbed by all parts of the tilapia.8. You

can now bake the fillets. At 400°F, it should be done in about 15 minutes or so. One way to know is if the tilapia has already turned completely white or if you can already be flaked evenly with a fork.

9. (Optional) You can also add grated Parmesan cheese to your tilapia fillets on the last 10 minutes of your baking time if you like.

10. Serve warm. Enjoy!

Broiled Halibut Fillets

The halibut has little oil and fat content and it is known for absorbing different flavours quite well. This fish tastes really good when you pair it with lemon and garlic.

Ingredients:

- 4 pcs. halibut fillets, measuring approximately 6 to 8 ounces each
- 3 tbsp. olive oil
- 3 cloves garlic, minced
- 2 tbsp. lemon juice
- ½ tsp. dried basil
- 1 tbsp. parsley, freshly chopped
- Salt and pepper
- Lemon slices and parsley leaves (optional)

Procedure:

1. Place halibut fillets on a greased baking sheet. Add salt and pepper.

2. Combine the olive oil, garlic, basil, and parsley in a saucepan. Keep the heat low. Heat the ingredients until the margarine has melted and the garlic has browned and softened.

3. Pour the mixture over the fillets. Make sure that all parts of the fish are well-coated by the mixture.

4. Heat the broiler and broil the fillets for approximately 10 minutes. During this time period, make sure to turn the fillets at least once.

5. Test with a fork to see if it's already done. It will flake away easily when you pierce it with a fork.6. Transfer cooked halibut on a plate. You may choose to garnish it with lemon slices and parsley leaves. Enjoy!

Baked Cajun Catfish

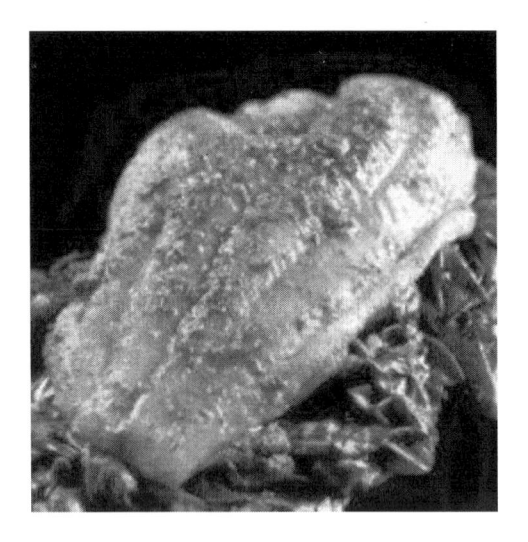

Aside from being a diabetic-friendly dish, the baked Cajun catfish gets a lot of compliments from visitors especially when the recipe is done to perfection!

Ingredients:

- 4 pcs. catfish fillets weighing approximately 8 ounces each
- 2 tbsp. olive oil
- 2 tsp. garlic salt
- 2 tsp. paprika
- 2 tsp. dried thyme
- ½ tsp. cayenne pepper
- ½ tsp. hot pepper sauce
- ¼ tsp. pepper powder

Procedure:

1. Using a small bowl, combine the olive oil, garlic salt, paprika, dried thyme, cayenne pepper, hot pepper sauce, and pepper powder. Mix thoroughly.

2. Brush the mixture over the fillets. Make sure you coat both sides.

3. Prepare a baking sheet and coat it with a cooking spray. Place fish on the baking sheet and bake the fillets at 450°F.

4. It should be done in 10 to 13 minutes. You can see it's done if you can already flake it easily with a fork.

5. Transfer on a plate and serve warm. Enjoy!

Poached Salmon

The poached salmon is a favourite among many because it is quite easy to prepare. In addition, it also doesn't make your house reek of fish after cooking and well, it's truly delicious! It's simply a good meal to serve to friends and family, whatever the occasion is.

Ingredients:

- 6 pcs. salmon fillets, measuring about 0.5 inches thick and weighing approximately 5 ounces each

- 2 cups dry white wine

- 2 cups water

- 6 peppercorns

- 1 pc. lemon, sliced

- 2 tbsp. fresh dill weed

- 1 celery stalk, chopped finely

- 1 pc. onion, sliced

- Salt to taste

Procedure:

1. Sprinkle a little salt on the salmon fillets.

2. On a large skillet, combine the white wine, water, peppercorns, lemon, dill, celery, and onion. Bring the combined ingredients to a boil. Cover the skillet and let it simmer on medium heat for around 10 minutes.

3. Place the salmon fillets on the skillet. Cook the salmon for 5 to 10 minutes. The cooking time will depend on the fillet's thickness, so you can check if it is done by seeing if it already flakes easily when pierced with a fork. Be careful not to overcook.

4. Transfer on a plate. Serve and enjoy!

Baked Salmon

Salmon is a real treat to have whether you are on a diet or not. It is packed with omega-3, has healthy proteins and amino acids, and is fairly easy to cook. This recipe calls for a marinade, so it requires a bit of time for the salmon to absorb the flavours. Alternately, you can prepare this ahead of time and just take it out when ready to cook.

Ingredients:

- 2 cloves, Garlic, minced

- 1-2 tablespoons Light Olive Oil

- 1 teaspoon Dried Basil

- 1 teaspoon Salt

- ½ teaspoon ground Black Pepper

- 1 tablespoon Lemon Juice

- 1 tablespoon fresh Parsley, chopped

- 2 (6ounce) Salmon Fillets

Procedure:

1. Prepare the marinade by mixing the minced garlic, olive oil, dried basil, salt, pepper, lemon juice, and parsley in a Ziploc bag.

2. Place the salmon fillets into the Ziploc bag with the marinade.

Refrigerate for at least an hour, making sure that all parts of the salmon are marinated well.

3. Pre-heat the oven to 375°F or 190°C.

4. Prepare an oven-safe dish.

5. When the salmon has been marinated, place over aluminium foil. Pour in the marinade to cover the salmon, and seal the foil.

6. Place the sealed salmon in the oven-safe dish and bake for 35-45minutes or until the meat is easily flaked with a fork.

7. Remove from oven. Enjoy.

Sesame-Crusted Tilapia

Another healthy way of serving tilapia is by baking it and infusing the fish with sesame oil flavours. Although it can be marinated 30 minutes before you plan to cook it, it is also recommended to marinate it overnight to let the flavours fully seep in.

Ingredients:

- 4 pcs. tilapia fillets, weighing around 6 ounces each
- 2 tbsp. lemon juice
- 2 tbsp. soy sauce (low sodium)
- 2 tbsp. ginger, minced
- 4 tsp. olive oil, divided
- 1 tsp. sesame oil, divided
- 2 tbsp. sesame seeds
- 1/3 cup chicken broth (low sodium)
- 3 cups green beans, approximately 12 ounces
- 1/8 tsp. salt
- 1/8 tsp. ground pepper

Procedure:

1. Pre-heat your oven to 425°F.

2. Using a small bowl, combine the lemon juice, soy sauce, 1 tbsp. ginger, 2 tsp. olive oil, and ½ tsp. sesame oil.

3. Prepare a flat baking sheet, lining it with a parchment paper or high quality aluminium foil. Place the tilapia fillets on the baking sheet, and coat them with lemon juice mixture.

4. Sprinkle the sesame seeds on the fillets evenly. Bake for about 8

minutes or until the tilapias flake easily.

5. While you're waiting for the tilapia to cook, heat 2 tsp. olive oil in a non-stick skillet over medium heat. Then, add the remaining ginger and sauté for 1 minute or until it smells good. Add the broth, beans, salt, and pepper. Cover the skillet and let it cook for 5 minutes, or until the beans turn bright green.

6. When done, turn off the stove and add ½ tsp. sesame oil. Mix well.

7. When the tilapia is ready, use a heat-proof spatula to transfer it onto a serving plate. Divide the green beans evenly among your guests. Enjoy!

Tilapia with Stewed Tomatoes and Spinach

There are many ways to cook tilapia, and if you are looking for a good side dish, spinach and stewed tomatoes would be perfect. This is a low-sodium dish that is easy to prepare, and you will surely score high on your guests because of its delicious taste and health benefits.

Ingredients:

- 4 pcs. tilapia fillets, approximately 6 to 8 ounces each
- 12 oz. whole canned tomatoes
- 4 mushrooms, sliced
- ½ pc. white onion, sliced
- 2 cloves of garlic
- 1 tsp. olive oil
- Spinach

Procedure:

1. In a frying pan, cook the onions using the olive oil. Add the mushroom and garlic and sauté until brown.

2. Add the canned tomatoes. Cook until it simmers.

3. Add the tilapia to the pan. Cook it for at least 3 minutes per side.

4. Put the spinach on top of the tilapia. Cover the pan and cook until the spinach wilts.

5. When the tilapia is cooked, transfer onto a plate and serve. Enjoy!

Tuna Burger

If you are looking for a healthy alternative to beef burgers, then the tuna fish burger is a highly recommended recipe. It has a lower fat content yet it doesn't compromise flavour.

Ingredients:

- 200 g tinned tuna in water, drained
- 60 mL teriyaki sauce
- 50 g breadcrumbs
- 1 egg white
- ¼ tsp. black pepper, ground
- ¼ tsp. garlic, minced
- ¼ tsp. hot pepper sauce
- ¼ tsp. olive oil

Procedure:

1. In a bowl, mix the tuna, breadcrumbs, teriyaki sauce, and egg whites until all of them are well combined. Make sure all ingredients can be rolled into a ball, with no large pieces of tuna remaining.

2. Add the black pepper, garlic, and hot pepper sauce to the mixture. Mix thoroughly until the condiments seem evenly distributed. Form two

patties afterwards.

3. In a frying pan, heat the olive oil over medium heat. Cook burgers for about 2 minutes each side, or until both sides are brown enough.

4. If you wish to make a sandwich, throw in some burger breads, lettuce, tomatoes, and cheese and you're good to go!

Tuna Salad

This tuna salad is very easy to prepare, healthy and tasty to boot as well. It makes an excellent snack on its own, but it can also be used as a sandwich filling. It goes really well with bread or crackers.

Ingredients:

- 200 g tinned tuna in water, flaked and drained
- 6 tbsp. salad dressing or mayonnaise
- 1 tbsp. grated Parmesan cheese
- 3 tbsp. sweet pickles
- 1/8 tsp. dried onion flakes
- 1 tbsp. dried parsley
- 1 tsp. dried dill
- 1 pinch garlic granules
- ¼ tsp. curry powder

Procedure:

1. In a medium-sized bowl, combine the tuna, mayonnaise or salad dressing, grated Parmesan cheese, and onion flakes. Mix thoroughly.

2. Season the combined ingredients with parsley, dill, curry powder, and garlic granules.

3. Use it as a sandwich filling or you can add bread or crackers as sides. Alternatively, you may choose to crush the crackers and mix it with the rest of the ingredients.

4. Serve and enjoy!

Salmon Burger

Aside from tuna, you can also make healthy burgers out of salmons. Combining it with herbs, breadcrumbs, and seasonings makes it an enjoyable afternoon snack or a light dinner. You may choose to make a sandwich or eat it with a salad on the side.

Ingredients:

- 450 g tinned salmon, flaked and drained

- 2 eggs

- 4 tbsp. fresh parsley, finely chopped

- 2 tbsp. onion, finely chopped

- 4 tbsp. breadcrumbs, seasoned dry
- 2 tbsp. lemon juice
- ½ tsp. dried basil
- 1 pinch chillies, crushed
- 1 tbsp. olive oil
- For the sauce:
- 2 tbsp. light mayonnaise
- 1 tbsp. lemon juice
- 1 pinch dried basil

Procedure:

1. In a medium-sized bowl, combine the salmon, eggs, onion, parsley, 2 tbsp. lemon juice, ½ tsp. basil, crushed chillies, and breadcrumbs. Mix thoroughly and form 6 pcs. burger patties measuring approximate 1.25 cm in thickness.

2. In a large frying pan, heat the olive oil over medium heat. Once the oil is hot enough, add the salmon burger patties and cook for about 4 minutes each side or until browned.

3. Mix the mayonnaise, 1 tbsp. lemon juice, and the basil on a small bowl. Spread on the burger patties. Serve and enjoy!

Ginger Lime Salmon

The ginger and lime salmon recipe is relatively easy to prepare and cook but it is still very tasty and appetizing. One of the best things about salmon is it can withstand and hold strong flavours really well. You can grill it or broil it, either way it will turn out great!

Ingredients:

- 2 pcs. salmon fillet, about 6 ounces each

- Mixed peppers, ringed and sliced

- Onion rings

- Marinade:

- ½ cup lime juice

- 1 tsp. fresh ginger, minced

- ½ tsp. garlic puree

- 1 tbsp. honey

Procedure:

1. Mix the ingredients for the marinade.

2. Put the salmon into the marinade mixture. Let it sit for a few hours. If you have plenty of time, you may want to do it overnight so the marinade will seep well into the salmon.

3. When the marinated salmon is ready to be cooked, pre-heat your oven to 425°F.

4. Fill the baking sheet with onion rings and mixed peppers. Place the salmon on top and pour the marinade.

5. Bake for approximately 20 to 25 minutes or until the salmon flakes easily with a fork. Serve warm and enjoy!

Mediterranean Fish Foil Pockets

This recipe gives you the opportunity to choose from a variety of fishes. Whatever you choose, your meal will surely come out healthy and tasty.

Ingredients:

- 1 lb. fish fillets, cut to 2 equal parts (cod, tuna, tilapia, or halibut)

- 2 tbsp. lemon juice

- ¼ cup black or kalamata olives, coarsely chopped and pitted
- 1 tbsp. fresh oregano, chopped
- 1 tbsp. extra-virgin olive oil
- 1 tbsp. capers, rinsed
- ½ tsp. ground pepper
- ½ tsp. salt, divided

Procedure:

1. Pre-heat your oven to 425°F.

2. Using a small bowl, combine the lemon juice, olives, oregano, olive oil, and capers.

3. Creating the foil pocket: Lay 2 sheets of foil on top of each other, measuring around 20 inches each. Coat the top layer with cooking spray, and then put one part of the fish at the centre of the foil. Add the salt and pepper, and then coat with the olive mixture you set aside earlier.

4. Bring the foil's short ends together. Make sure you leave enough room to get the food steamed and cooked. Fold the foil and seal with a pinch. The seams must be sealed tightly so that the steam will not escape.

5. Bake the foil pockets in your oven for around 20 minutes or so.

6. Be careful when you take the foil out of the oven as it is very hot. Open the foil pocket to let the steam escape. Transfer the fish to a plate using a heat-proof spatula. Serve and enjoy!

Fish Gyros with Tzatziki Sauce

If you are looking for a healthy and yet heavy snack, you can't go wrong with fish gyros with tzatziki sauce. This recipe gives you an exciting and easy way to experiment with fish, yogurt, and herbs as main ingredients.

Ingredients:

- 1 lb. cod or tilapia fillets

- 4 leaves Boston lettuce

- 1 clove garlic, minced

- ¼ tsp. crushed red pepper

- ¼ cup cilantro, fresh and minced

- Salt, pepper, coriander (ground), to taste

Tzatziki Sauce:

- 2 cups non-fat plain yogurt

- 1 medium-sized cucumber, seeded, peeled, shredded, and squeezed dry

- 2 cloves garlic, minced
- 1 tbsp. extra-virgin olive oil
- 1 tbsp. red wine vinegar
- 1 tbsp. fresh thyme (alternatively, 1 ½ tsp. dried thyme)
- 2 tsp. lemon juice
- ¼ tsp. salt

Procedure for the Sauce:

1. Combine all the sauce ingredients in a bowl.

2. Transfer in a container with a cover and refrigerate for one hour. If you have time, you can let it sit overnight.

Procedure for the Fish Gyros:

1. Pre-heat your oven to 375°F.2. Season the fish fillets with garlic, red pepper, cilantro, salt, and coriander. Bake for approximately 10 minutes or until the fish flakes easily.

3. Lay a large leaf of Boston lettuce on a plate. Transfer the fish onto the plate and pour over the tzatziki sauce. Serve warm and enjoy!

Lemon and Dill Salmon

The lemon and dill salmon is a favourite among many home cooking enthusiasts because it only takes a few ingredients and a little time to cook and prepare. You can also your favourite herbs and capers to add a personal touch to this simple recipe.

Ingredients:

- 1 lb. wild salmon fillets

- 1 pc. lemon

- 1 tsp. dill

- Olive oil

- Salt and pepper, to taste

Procedure:

1. Pre-heat your oven to 375°F.

2. Prepare your baking sheet and line with parchment paper or high quality aluminum foil.

3. Lay salmon on the baking sheet. Lightly coat the fillets with olive oil.

Sprinkle evenly with salt, pepper and dill.

4. Slice the lemon into thin pieces and place it on top of the salmon.

5. Bake it for about 20 minutes or until the salmon can be easily flaked.

Serve with your favourite vegetables on the side. Enjoy!

Seasoned Tilapia

Many people like cooking the tilapia because you can basically do a lot of things with it. Another easy recipe for this fish is the seasoned tilapia, which only requires you to have some of the most commonly used condiments in the kitchen. In addition to the tilapia, of course!

Ingredients:

- 4 pcs. tilapia fillets

- 1 tbsp. extra-virgin olive oil

- 3 cloves garlic, minced

- 1 tsp. ginger

- 1 tsp. paprika

- 1 tsp. black pepper, ground

- 1 tsp. dried mustard

- 1 tsp. oregano

- 1 tsp. chilli powder

- 1 pinch cayenne pepper

Procedure:

1. Pre-heat your oven to 400°F.

2. Prepare a flat baking sheet and line it with parchment paper.

3. Combine the paprika, ginger, ground black pepper, dried mustard, oregano, chilli powder, and cayenne pepper in a medium-sized bowl.

4. Coat each fillet lightly with olive oil. Sprinkle the combined seasonings

and garlic and place the fish on the baking sheet.

5. Bake for about 10 minutes or until the salmon flakes easily. Serve and

enjoy!

Snacks

Buffalo Chicken Tenders

This is an easy recipe for an all-time favourite.

Ingredients:

- 1 lb. Chicken Breasts

- 2 tablespoons Olive Oil

- ¼ cup Hot Sauce

Procedure:

1. Cut the chicken breasts into strips.

2. Combine the olive oil and the hot sauce in a zip lock bag, then add the

chicken strips and let it marinate for at least 30minutes.

3. Pre-heat oven to 375°F.

4. Place the chicken strips in an oven-safe dish and pour remaining marinade over the pieces.

5. Bake in the pre-heated oven for 12-16 minutes or until cooked through.

6. Serve and enjoy!

If you are in a hurry, you can just let it marinate for however long you can wait, then cook immediately. Longer marinating time only allows the chicken to absorb more of the heat from the hot sauce. You can serve this with more hot sauce or some celery sticks on the side.

Cauliflower Popcorn

Who ever said that healthy ingredients cannot be eaten as snacks? Here is a simple and healthy 'popcorn' recipe to make you think otherwise.

Ingredients:

- 1 head Cauliflower
- 4 tablespoons Olive Oil
- 1 teaspoon Salt

Procedure:

1. Pre-heat the oven to 425°F.

2. Remove the stem from the cauliflower and cut the heads into individual pieces the size of ping-pong balls. Be careful not to cut them too small.

3. Combine the olive oil and the salt in a large bowl, then whisk together.

4. Toss in the cauliflower heads into the olive oil and mix to coat all of the pieces.

5. Transfer the cauliflower onto an oven-safe dish and bake in the pre-heated oven for about 1hour. Make sure to turn the pieces over from time to time to let it cook on all sides.

6. Serve immediately and enjoy!

You can also add fat-free parmesan cheese, garlic powder, or any seasoning of your choice for an added flavour.

Chicken Lettuce Wraps

Even if you are on a diet, you can enjoy tasty snacks like these chicken lettuce wraps. You can even prepare this ahead of time and serve to guests or family and friends.

Ingredients:

- 1 Chicken Breast
- 1 Scallion, diced
- ½ cup Red Grapes, chopped
- 2 tablespoons Celery, chopped
- 1 tablespoon Olive Oil
- Salt and Pepper to taste
- 1 pack Iceberg Lettuce Leaves

Procedure:

1. Bake the chicken breasts for about 30minutes in 350°F or until cooked through.
2. Cut the chicken breasts into small cubes.
3. In a bowl, combine the diced scallions, chopped grapes, celery, olive oil, and salt and pepper, then add the chicken pieces.
4. Refrigerate until chilled.
5. To serve, take one lettuce leaf at a time, spoon the chicken mixture into the center, then wrap the lettuce around the chicken mixture.

Enjoy!

Egg Salad Wraps

Just because Cycle 1 does not allow you to eat bread does not mean you can no longer enjoy your favourite sandwich recipes. Here is a classic egg sandwich with lettuce leaves instead of bread. Yummy and healthy!

Ingredients:

- 2 Eggs, hardboiled
- Salt and Pepper to taste
- 2 tablespoons Fat-free Yogurt
- Lettuce Leaves

Procedure:

1. Take the hardboiled eggs and mash them up with a fork.

2. Add the mayonnaise, and then sprinkle with salt and pepper. Mix everything properly.

3. When ready to eat, get a lettuce leaf, place a spoonful of the egg mixture in the middle, then wrap the lettuce around the egg.

4. Enjoy!

If the yogurt is too strong for you, you can simply substitute with some olive oil and a dash of vinegar.

Mock Mashed Potatoes

If you find yourself craving for mashed potatoes, try this recipe out so that you still stick to your diet. Enjoy!

Ingredients:

- 1 head Cauliflower

- 2 tablespoons Non-fat Yogurt

- ¼ teaspoon Garlic Powder

- ¼ teaspoon Onion Powder

- ¼ teaspoon Salt

Procedure:

1. Remove the hard stem of the cauliflower and cut into smaller pieces.

2. Steam the cauliflower until very soft.

3. Mash the cauliflower, and then add the yogurt and the seasonings.

4. Mix well and enjoy!

You can also use your favourite seasonings or adjust to your preferred taste.

Stuffed Mushrooms

Stuffed mushrooms are great snacks that are both filling and delicious. The best thing about this recipe is that it lets you keep on course with your diet while still letting you enjoy flavourful snacks.

Ingredients:

- 1 lb. Whole Mushrooms

- 2 pcs. Tomatoes, diced

- ½ cup Ground Turkey

- Salt and Pepper to taste

- ¼ cup Fat-free Mozzarella or Parmesan Cheese

Procedure:

1. Pre-heat oven to 350°F.

1. Clean the whole mushrooms and remove the middle.

2. In a bowl, mix together the ground turkey and the diced tomatoes. Season with salt and pepper.

3. Stuff the mushrooms with the ground turkey mixture and place on an oven-safe dish.

4. Top the stuffed mushrooms with mozzarella or parmesan cheese, then bake in the pre-heated oven for 15-20minutes or until the mushrooms have softened and the cheese begins to brown.

5. Serve and enjoy!

Cholesterol Lowering Diet

Lower Cholesterol with Paleo Recipes and Low Carb

Introduction

Having cholesterol levels that are higher than normal puts you at risk for cardiovascular disease. High cholesterol levels in the blood will eventually lead to clogged arteries that can cause a blockage to the heart or to the brain. If these arteries become clogged, it can produce a stroke or a heart attack. If a person is diagnosed with high cholesterol and does not change their diet the high cholesterol will have detrimental effects on their health. If you do nothing about your cholesterol and it is highly possible a stroke or heart attack will happen in the future. Dieting is one of the best ways to correct high cholesterol and both the low carb and the Paleolithic diet plans are excellent to help lower the cholesterol naturally.

Many physicians and health care providers agree that the first line of action when the blood cholesterol levels are elevated is to change the diet. Dieting alone can often lower the cholesterol levels back to normal. Low carb foods, which are found in the low carb diet and the Paleolithic diet, are the right foods to eat to help the body to bring the cholesterol levels back to normal. Both of the diets feature foods that are lean meats (high proteins) and fresh fruits and vegetables, in particular green leafy vegetables. If you are accustomed to a diet of high carbs it means you probably have an addiction to junk food. Junk foods are high in carbs and contain a lot of sugar and empty calories. A junk food diet will help to raise cholesterol levels.

The body needs fiber to help cleanse the body and lower the cholesterol. Both the low carb diet and the Paleolithic diet have the fiber from fruits and vegetables. Fiber from vegetables is one of the best ways the body can receive this necessary nutrient.

Most of the foods included in the low carb diet plan and the Paleolithic diet plan are considered "super foods." These are foods that highly nutritious and help the body to function better, including maintaining a better cholesterol level. "Good" fats, which make up a large portion of the low carb diet plan, help the body to have a stronger immune system and be better able to fight off the illnesses caused by high cholesterol.

If you have been diagnosed with high cholesterol and your health care provider encouraged you to try dieting and changing your diet to lower the cholesterol levels you may want to show them this book. Let them see the recipes included in the low carb diet plan and the Paleolithic diet plan and ask them if the foods included in the book are ones that will help your body to lower your cholesterol levels naturally. Chances are they will say yes and give you their seal of approval on both of diets as good diets to help lower your cholesterol.

It is wise when dieting to lower cholesterol to make the diet a permanent lifestyle change. You will find so many recipes within this book between the low carb diet plan and the Paleolithic diet plan that you can plan the meals for weeks without repeating the dishes. There are even healthy snack and dessert recipes.

When going on a diet to help improve a health condition it is important to stick with the diet plan and not cheat. With all the wonderful recipes in this book, there is no reason to cheat. You can find recipes that probably include all your favorite (healthy) foods. If you have a strong addiction to junk food, you need to break that bad habit. By feeding your body nutritious foods from the low carb diet plan and the Paleolithic diet plan, you are helping your body to break the junk food habit. Before too much longer you will no longer crave the junk and instead you will want to eat the healthy foods.

Ironically, skipping meals is not a good idea if you are attempting to become healthier. Your body needs food for the energy to be able to function. When cholesterol levels are high, the body needs the right foods to help bring the cholesterol levels back down to a normal reading. Eat breakfast, lunch, and supper and include snacks in between the meals. Eat small to moderate sized meals, avoid over stuffing. Avoid eating out of habit and only eat when the body feels hungry.

By choosing recipes from this book, from the low carb and the Paleolithic diet plans, you are giving your body the best foods it needs to help heal and strengthen the immune system, which will in turn help the body to regulate the cholesterol levels. You can do more research and find out how "low carb diets help to reduce cholesterol levels." Remember both of the sections in this book are low carb so you are giving your body the best chance to be healthy.

Stick with the diet plan to help lower the cholesterol levels. The food you eat may be responsible for your elevated cholesterol levels. Smoking will also raise the cholesterol levels. Genetics also plays a role in some people for elevated levels. No matter where you fall, if your cholesterol is on the rise you must stop your bad habits, quit smoking, and eat better. It is much better for the body if dieting alone can lower the levels. If not, there are prescription medications, but they do come with risks. Do all you can before going on medications to lower your cholesterol naturally.

Always clear your diet plan with your health care provider. The low carb diet and the Paleolithic diet both show promise to help start and maintain a healthy eating lifestyle. Both of the diets have helped others to lower their cholesterol naturally if they stuck with the diet plan. Take your health care provider's advice with your health, especially if they suggested a change in your diet. When you receive a high cholesterol reading, normally you can diet for a couple of months to help bring it down. Keep the diet changes you make and keep your cholesterol levels normal.

Section 1: Low Carb Diet

Low calorie diet is a general phrase that can have different meanings. Anyone can eat smaller portions of the same foods they are already consuming, but this doesn't adequately justify a low calorie diet. What you eat makes a huge difference in getting the most out of any type of diet. Advertising trends can misrepresent the true meaning of a low calorie diet, while staying within certain truthful perimeters. This book is designed to bring focus on true low calorie diets, that introduce you to a new way of life. Being stronger, healthier and having more energy, is the goal of a successful low calorie diet.

There will be misconceptions addressed, as you read through the chapters. Facts about preservatives, sugar, grains and drinks, will awaken your thoughts about what you are feeding yourself, and your family. The truth is, a low calorie diet is not just for losing weight, but learning how all foods have a direct effect on your body. Just as you know that cigarettes and large amounts of alcohol are harmful, habits of eating certain foods can weaken you immune system, slow down metabolism, and cause fatty tissue to form in your arteries and veins.

You will also find delicious recipes that are just right for stepping into your new life. If you wish to shed a few pounds, mix and match the recipes and portions, according to the carbs. With each recipe made from low-carb foods, and under 500 calories each, the choices are huge.

Why Calorie Counting is a Lie

Keeping calories low should not involve taking out a book and writing down every calorie of food you eat. That gets real boring, real fast. You simply need to know what types of foods can easily be burned off and which ones, cannot. One of the highest forms of calories that is difficult to unload, is sugar. Look at any label and you will see this word.

According to the American Heart Association, no more than 100 calories of sugar should make up a grown woman's diet in one day. This amounts to 6 teaspoons. For a man, 150 calories, or 9 teaspoons, should be the limit. One bowl of whole-grain cereal with milk, contains as much as 9 teaspoons of sugar.

While this may seem downhearted, it gets even worse. Preservatives play a very important role in adding empty calories and high carbs. Take, for example, a box of macaroni and cheese. You may feel that you are being frugal in selecting a product that has cheese, grain, and vitamins, not to mention a shelf life of a year, but here is the ugly truth. Preservatives contain corn syrup, hydrogenated oil, nitrates or sulfates. While consumption of these ingredients can give you a sensation of fullness, they are very difficult for the digestive system to process. Feeling sluggish, developing heart burn and producing fat, are three real symptoms of consuming processed foods. While the package calories may read, 400 calories per serving, is doesn't tell you that these calories are close to impossible to burn off.

You can make it a habit of counting calories, but unless you start with foods that are good for your body, consuming a low carb diet, will be in vein.

Chapter 1: Rise and Shine with a Fortified Breakfast

Crunchy Maple Grape Nuts

Description

Breakfast should contain energy-packed foods to jump start your day. However, in the hustle and bustle of preparing for the day, many people grab a box of cereal. Instead of breaking this habit, keep your own homemade varieties on hand. Low calorie and delicious, these recipes will give your family the right mix of vitamins in a low carb diet. Make ahead and store in airtight containers.

Yields: 12 Servings

Ingredients

3 cups whole wheat flour
1/2 cup barley flour
1/3 cup oat flour
1/3 cup toasted wheat germ
1/2 cup brown sugar
1/2 teaspoon salt
2 teaspoons baking soda
2 teaspoons maple flavoring
1/4 cup heated honey or maple syrup
1/2 cup low-fat milk
2 teaspoons cinnamon

Instructions

1. Warm oven to 325 degrees.

2. Sift and blend dry ingredients

3. In a separate bowl, beat the liquid ingredients together.

4. Stir liquid ingredients into dry ingredients.

5. If the mixture is too watery, work in additional flour.

6, Spread on 2 or 3 baking sheets and bake for 10-15 minutes. After baking, allow to cool, then break up any large clumps and return to oven for an additional 10 minutes.

7. Cool and store in air-tight container.

Healthy Honey Oat Cereal

Description

Here is another version of homemade cereal for those that love to wake up their mouths with lots of crunch and flavor. Nuts, raisins and sweet natural ingredients make this breakfast cereal a great kick start to the day.

Yields: 12 Servings

Ingredients

4 1/2 cups rolled oats
6 Tablespoons sunflower seeds
12 Tablespoons sliced almonds
6 Tablespoons chopped pecans
6 Tablespoons raisins
6 Tablespoons honey
1/4 teaspoon cinnamon
1/4 teaspoon maple extract

Instructions

1. Warm oven to 325 degrees.

2. Place a small pan over a larger pan of boiling water and add the honey, cinnamon and extract. Heat just until well mixed.

3. Spread baking sheet with aluminum foil and combine all other ingredients (except raisins). You may want to use a baking pan that has a slight lip around the sides, or raise up the edges of the foil to keep dry ingredients from falling off.

4. Using your hands, or a large wooden spoon, mix well, the dry ingredients.

5. Add the honey mixture and coat as much of the dry ingredients as you can.

6. Spread the mixture evenly over the pan and bake for 15 minutes.

7. Remove from oven and let cool. Do not worry if your cereal does not appear crunchy. This comes once it has cooled.

9. After cooling, mix in the raisins and store in an airtight container.

French Toast Strawberry Dippers

Description

Getting kids to the breakfast table is a tough chore. Usually running late, they will grab a finger food, like a doughnut or other gluten-filled treat. Have these quick dippers ready to reach for as they hit the door, and know that they are getting good taste and healthy energy.

Yields: 4 Servings

Ingredients

8 slices low-carb sandwich white bread
4 Tablespoons softened cream cheese
6 fresh, sliced strawberries
3 large eggs
1/4 cup low-fat milk
1 Tablespoon butter
1/2 cup maple syrup
1/4 cup no-sugar strawberry jam

Instructions

1. Spread cream cheese on 4 slices of bread.

2. Line the cream cheese topping with the sliced strawberries.

3. Top with a bread slice to make a sandwich.

4. In a bowl, mix together the eggs and milk.

5. Use 1/2 of the butter to lightly grease a griddle or skillet and heat on medium.

6. Dip the sandwiches into the egg batter, one at a time, and place in the warmed griddle or skillet.

7. Cook the bread on each side until golden brown. Add remaining butter, if needed.

8. Remove each sandwich, pat with paper towels and cut into 4 long sections.

9. Combine the syrup and jam and heat in a microwave for 30 seconds.

10. Remove and stir well.

11. Place the tasty toast sections in a bread basket, beside the dip, and watch them disappear.

Breakfast Egg Muffins

Description

Use the weekend to cook up a filling and healthy egg breakfast for the day ahead. It will soon become a tradition of a starting a free day, just right, with plenty to go around.

Yields: 8 Servings

Ingredients

8 eggs
½ cup Swiss or Cheddar cheese
½ cup milk
¼ cup chopped onion
¼ cup chopped mushrooms
¼ cup green pepper
¼ cup chopped tomatoes
2 Tablespoons butter
4 plain bagels
8 stale pieces of bread

Instructions

1. Lay out the pieces of bread and cut out the middle in the shape of a circle. This will serve as a pattern for cooking your egg mixture.

2. In a bowl, whisk the eggs and milk together.

3. Blend in the onion, mushrooms, green pepper and tomatoes.

4. Melt 1 Tablespoon butter in a large skillet and arrange the bread patterns.

5. Pour the egg mixture in the center of each bread pattern, lower heat and cover.

6. After about 4 minutes, remove the cover and sprinkle each round egg with cheese.

7. Add extra butter if needed to keep the bottoms from sticking.

7. Turn off heat and recover skillet.

8. Toast ½ bagel and place on a plate.

9. Carefully remove each egg and peel away the outer bread.

10. Place the round egg on top of the bagel, discarding the bread.

Serve with fresh fruit or a glass of juice.

Cinnamon Raisin Muffins

Description

Nothing can compare to fresh, homemade muffins, right from the oven. These treats will satisfy your craving for bread and sweets, but actually give you less than 150 calories each. Vary the ingredients and have a different selection of muffins each week.

Yields: 12 Servings

Ingredients

1 ½ cups flour
1 ½ teaspoons baking powder
½ teaspoon baking soda
¼ cup butter, refrigerated
1 egg
¼ cup sour cream
¼ cup milk
¼ cup raisins
2 Tablespoons sugar, or sugar substitute
1 teaspoon cinnamon

Instructions

1. Heat oven to 400 degrees F.

2. Combine flour, baking powder and baking soda in large bowl.

3. Cut in the butter until coarse crumbs form.

4. Make a well in the center.

5. In a small bowl, beat the egg, then add the sour cream, milk, raisins, sugar and cinnamon, blending thoroughly.

6. Pour the egg mixture in the center of the flour and mix well.

7. Take a muffin pan and either line with paper muffin holders, or grease lightly.

8. Fill each cup 2/3 full.

9. Bake for 15 minutes, or until browned.

Apple butter or fruit preserves can be used to spread on each muffin.

Asparagus and Mushroom Omelet

Description

This dish makes a meaty and tasty meal for not only breakfast, but lunch, as well. With only 5 grams of carbohydrates and 21 grams of protein, per serving, you will pick up extra energy and not get hungry through the course of the day.

Yields: 4 Servings

Ingredients

8 eggs
8 Tablespoons water
12 stalks fresh asparagus
1 cup sliced mushrooms
1 cup low-fat mozzarella cheese

Instructions

1. In a large skillet, add an inch of water and bring to a boil.

2. Add the asparagus, in two or three different sections, and cook uncovered, just until tender-crisp. Remove and pat dry.

3. Using a large bowl, whisk the eggs and water.

4. Prepare a large skillet by melting 1 Tablespoon butter .

5. When butter reaches a sizzle over medium-high heat, add ½ of the egg mixture.

6. Cook until the bottom of the egg mixture sets.

7. Carefully lift up the edges with a spatula and allow the uncooked portion to flow out and cook.

8. Once the top is cooked thoroughly, add the asparagus, mushrooms and cheese, and fold into a sandwich with part of the egg.

9. Remove the omelet and cut in half. Repeat with the rest of the egg mixture.

Chapter 2: Lunchtime Recipes for Afternoon Energy

Eggs, Lox and Caramelized Onions on Bagel

Description

Afternoons do not have to be a battle with fatigue and a sluggish feeling. Allow your mid-day meal to recharge your body with fulfilling foods that bring nutrition to your organs and pep up your blood flow. You'll never miss the calories, but you will enjoy missing that afternoon slump that used to slow you down.

Yields: 4 Servings

Ingredients

4 teaspoons butter
1 sliced onion
8 eggs
2 Tablespoons heavy cream
4 ounces lox
4 toasted buns

Instructions

1. Melt 2 teaspoons butter in a skillet, add sliced onions, and cook over medium heat for 8-10 minutes, or until golden brown. Remove to a plate.

2. Beat eggs and cream in a bowl.

3. Melt remaining butter in the skillet and add mixture from bowl.

4. Add salt and pepper, to flavor, and stir constantly, until almost set.

5. Add lox and onions, stirring until heated throughout.

6. Spread on toasted bagel halves.

Silky Onion Soup

Description

Enjoy this tasty soup with a few carrot sticks and a piece of Melba toast. The creamy rich flavor will remind you of an elegant evening meal, instead of a lunch time treat.

Yields: 8 Servings

Ingredients

3 Tablespoons butter
1 sliced onion
2 garlic cloves, minced
2 leeks (white part only), cut in 1/2" strips
1 medium zucchini, sliced
½ teaspoon tarragon
¼ teaspoon salt
¼ teaspoon pepper
2 cups scallions, thinly sliced
28 ounces chicken broth
1 ½ cup water
½ cup heavy cream

Instructions

1. Melt 2 Tablespoons butter in a saucepan, over medium heat.

2. Add onion, garlic, leeks, zucchini, tarragon, salt and pepper.

3. Cover and simmer about 7 minutes
4. Stir in 1 ¾ cup scallions and cook until wilted.

5. Add broth and water and increase the heat until all is boiling.

6. Reduce heat and simmer for 10 minutes.

7. Remove from heat and break up the vegetables with a masher.

8. Return to a medium heat and add the remaining butter and the cream.

9. Heat just until boiling begins.

10. Remove from heat and sprinkle with remaining scallions.

Makes a great make ahead meal for warming up when on the run.

Tuna Salad Supreme in Tortilla Shells

Description

Give new meaning to tired tuna salad that grows old after a time or two. The right mix of veggies and a complementary bowl will turn tuna into a sought after lunch.

Yields: 4 Servings

Ingredients

4 8-inch round flour tortillas
1 Tablespoon olive oil
3 5-ounce cans Albacore tuna, drained
6 stalks celery, chopped
1 cucumber, peeled and cubed
2/3 cup mayonnaise
16 cherry tomatoes, quartered
4 lettuce leaves

Instructions

1. Heat oven to 400-degrees.

2. Take 4 oven-proof bowls and turn upside down.

3. Brush both sides of the tortillas with olive oil and place one over each bowl.

4. Bake in the oven until the tortillas are crisp and hold their shape, about 7 to 10 minutes.

5. Remove from oven and keep draped over the bowls until completely cooled.

6. In a bowl, mix the remaining ingredients (except the lettuce leaves).

7. Invert the bowls and lace each one with a lettuce leaf before adding the tuna salad.

You will never eat tuna salad on bread again!

Low-Cal Greek Salad

Description

Never miss out on the taste of feta cheese, blended perfectly in a luscious bed of romaine lettuce. Here is a great way to give in to your taste bud desires, without adding unwanted carbohydrates.

Yields: 1 Serving

Ingredients

8 leaves romaine lettuce, torn
1 cucumber, peeled and sliced
1 chopped tomato
½ cup red onion, sliced
½ cup low-fat feta cheese, crumbled
2 Tablespoons olive oil
2 Tablespoons fresh lemon juice
1 teaspoon dried oregano leaves
½ teaspoon salt

Instructions

1. Mix torn lettuce, cucumber, tomato, onion, and cheese in a large serving bowl.

2. Using a separate bowl, whisk together the oil, lemon juice, oregano, and salt.

3. Pour over salad.

Spinach Salad with Chicken and Raspberry

Description

Raspberry adds a tangy flavor to salads and chicken, so why not combine them? Adding a few other tricks will make this mid-day meal something to look forward to.

Yields: 4 Servings

Ingredients

¼ cup white vinegar
5 Tablespoons olive oil
1 teaspoon honey
½ teaspoon orange peel, shredded
½ teaspoon salt
¼ teaspoon pepper
4 skinless, boneless chicken breast halves
5 cups torn spinach
5 cups torn mixed greens
1 cup fresh raspberries
1 papaya, peeled, seeded and cubed

Instructions

1. Combine the vinegar, 4 Tablespoons olive oil, honey, orange peel, salt and pepper.

2. Pour into an airtight jar and shake well. Store in the refrigerator to chill.

3. In a large skillet, heat over medium heat and add the remaining oil .

4. Add the chicken breasts and cook for 10 to 15 minutes, turning often, to brown all sides.

5. When no longer pink, remove from the skillet and pat out any excess oil and water.

6. Cut the warm chicken into thin strips.

7. In a large bowl, toss the greens, spinach and chicken strips.

8. Take your salad dressing and pour over the salad, tossing well.

9. Add the raspberries and cubed papaya, tossing gently.

Lettuce Roll-Ups with Pumpkin Seed Pate

Description

Move over hamburgers. This flavorful rendition of what used to be a sandwich, will make you wonder why anyone would choose meat over fresh veggies. Filled with marinated vegetables and seasoned with a unique pate, all your friends will want your recipe.

Yields: 6 Servings

Ingredients

6 large lettuce leaves

Marinated Vegetables:

2 stalks celery, sliced in 2-inch strips
1 cup carrots, shredded
¼ cup red onion, thinly sliced
2 Tablespoons flax oil
2 teaspoons lemon juice

Pate:

1 ½ garlic cloves
juice from 1 squeezed lemon
1 cup pumpkin seeds, soaked and sprouted
¼ cup flax oil
¾ teaspoon salt
¼ cup fresh parsley
¼ cup fresh basil
¼ cup dill
1/8 teaspoon turmeric
½ teaspoon fresh rosemary

Instructions for Pate

1. Using a food processor, place the garlic and pumpkins seeds inside and chop.

2. Add the lemon juice and mix until creamy.

3. Add the herbs and seasonings.

4. Pulse to finely chop all the herbs.

5. Spoon into a bowl.

Instructions for Assembly

1. Place all ingredients for marinated vegetables in a medium bowl and coat all pieces.

2. Lay flat a lettuce leaf and spread on a generous amount of pate.

3. Add ½ cup of marinated vegetables.

4. Roll up, folding the top and bottom to secure.

Chapter 3: Great Dinner Surprises

Mushroom Laced Meatballs

Description

You don't have to tell the family that they are on a low calorie diet when serving up dishes that are guaranteed to hit the spot. Lean hamburger will be anything, but boring, when dressed up with the right spices. See if anyone believes you when you admit that this dish has only 300 calories per serving.

Yields: 6 Servings

Ingredients

1 pound ground beef
1 egg
1/2 cup whole wheat bread crumbs
4 ounces shredded cheddar cheese
1/4 cup onion, chopped
1 Tablespoon Worcestershire sauce
1 Tablespoon fresh parsley, chopped
1/2 teaspoon basil
1/2 teaspoon pepper
1 Tablespoon oil
1 cup sliced mushrooms
1/2 cup beef broth
1/2 cup cooking wine

Instructions

1. Mix together meat, egg, bread crumbs, cheese, onion, Worcestershire sauce, parsley, basil and pepper.

2. Shape into 12 meatballs.

3. Add oil to skillet and brown meatballs on all sides, about 5 minutes.

4. Remove meatballs and dry on paper towels.

5. Add mushrooms to the drippings in the skillet and cook over medium heat for 2 to 3 minutes.

6. In a small bowl, mix flour, broth and wine until blended.

7. Pour over mushrooms and cook until boiling, stirring constantly.

8. Turn down heat and simmer sauce for 2 minutes.

9. Add meatballs to the creamy mixture and warm thoroughly, before serving.

Sassy Cheese and Chicken Enchiladas

Description

Kids will come running when they smell the succulent aroma of one of their favorite meals. Chicken enchiladas always top the favorites list, especially when dripping with cheese sauce. Microwave the entire meal and save time.

Yields: 6 Servings

Ingredients

2 cups cooked chicken breasts, chopped
1/2 cup chopped onion
1 garlic clove, minced
1 Tablespoon oil
4 ounces chopped green chilies
1/2 cup chicken broth
2 teaspoons chili powder
1 teaspoon cumin
4 ounces cubed cream cheese
6 6-inch flour tortillas
1/4 pound Colby or Cheddar cheese, cubed
2 Tablespoons milk
1/2 cup fresh chopped tomato

Instructions

1. In a 2-quart microwavable dish, mix onion, garlic and oil.

2. Microwave on high for 2 minutes. Stir and return for 1 more minute.

3. Remove and add chicken, chilies, broth and seasonings. Blend well.

4. Return to microwave and cook on high for 4 minutes.

5. Remove and add cream cheese, stirring until all the cheese is melted.

6. Spoon 1/2 cup of the mixture onto a tortilla shell and roll up. Repeat 6 times and place all, seam side down, on a flat microwavable dish.

7. In a clean microwavable dish, mix the Colby or Cheddar cheese, milk and 1/4 cup tomato and microwave on high for 1 minute. Stir and return for another 1 or 2 minutes.

8. Remove the cheese sauce and pour over the enchiladas.

9. Microwave on high for 4 minutes.

10. Remove and top with remaining tomatoes.

11. Return to the microwave and cook on high for another 2 to 3 minutes.

Serve with salsa and chips.

Colorful Veggie Meatloaf

Description

Put sparkle in an old dish by using creative, and healthy vegetables. This one dish meal will add new meaning to meatloaf, as it was once known.

Yields: 8 Servings

Ingredients

1 1/2 pounds lean ground beef
3 cups white bread crumbs, toasted
1 cup diced tomatoes
1 cup fresh or frozen green beans (thawed)
1 egg
1 carrot
2 Tablespoons Worcestershire sauce
1 1/2 teaspoons salt
1/4 teaspoon pepper
1/4 cup ketchup

Instructions

1. Preheat oven to 375 degrees F
2. In a large bowl, mix all ingredients (except ketchup), until well blended.

3. Turn into a loaf pan and top with ketchup.

4. Bake for 50 to 60 minutes, or until cooked throughout.

5. Remove and transfer to a platter, patting dry any excess fat.

Serve with a tossed salad for a filling, low calorie dinner.

Grilled Summer Kabobs

Description

Grilling during the spring and summer months can be exciting. The smell of meat that is char-broiled to perfection, can get your tummy growling. Make a delightful and low carb dinner, while including steak. A little bit goes a long way with this recipe.

Yields: 6 Servings

Ingredients

1 1/2 pounds boneless beef sirloin steak, cut into strips
1 zucchini, cut in 1-inch pieces
1 squash, cut into diagonal pieces
2 onions, quartered
12 cherry tomatoes
1/2 cup mayonnaise
1/2 cup plain yogurt
1/4 cup lemon juice
3 cloves garlic, minced
2 teaspoons minced ginger root
1/2 teaspoon cardamom
1/2 teaspoon cumin
1/2 teaspoon coriander
1/8 teaspoon red pepper

Instructions

1. Prepare the marinade by blending all seasonings, mayonnaise, yogurt and lemon juice. Put 1/2 cup of dressing aside for later.

2. Skewer the steak strips between the zucchini, squash, onions, and tomatoes.

3. Place the kabobs on a hot grill and brush with the marinade.

4. Grill for 10 or 15 minutes, or until the meat reaches the required doneness, turning and brushing twice.

5. Remove and serve with the reserved dressing.

Veggie Laced Macaroni and Cheese

Description

Macaroni and Cheese, from a box, offers little in the way of low carbs and vitamins. However, it will not take long for family to miss this simple mix of cheese and pasta. Try this homemade version that has a new twist and watch them ask for more.

Yields: 4 Servings

Ingredients

9 ounces penne noodles
1 ½ cups sharp cheddar cheese
1 Tablespoon tarragon
1/8 teaspoon ground white pepper
4 carrots, peeled and sliced
juice from one fresh orange
¼ cup water

Instructions

Warm oven to 350 degrees F.

In a saucepan, combine the carrots and juice from orange.

Add I/4 cup water and heat until boiling.

Turn down, cover and simmer for about 30 minutes.

Remove from heat and transfer to a blender.

Puree contents.

In a separate pan, boil the penne noodles in salted water until al dente.

Drain off the water, reserving 1 cup in the pan.

Add the drained pasta to the pan, along with the puree.

Heat on medium, stirring to coat penne.

Cook, stirring often,
Add 1 cup cheese, tarragon and white pepper.

Once the mixture becomes creamy, pour all into a greased baking dish.

Add the remaining cheese on top and bake for 20 minutes.

Remove and let stand for 5 minutes before serving.

Chapter 4: Unique Side Dishes

Fake Mashed Potatoes

Description

If your family craves meat and potatoes, this is just an old habit. However, you can give them what they want by serving a meat dish and using this unique recipe for mashed potatoes, made from fresh cauliflower. The flavor will be better, the consistency, fluffy, and that mindset of meat and potatoes will quickly dissipate.

Yields: 4 Servings

Ingredients

1 fresh cauliflower head
1 Tablespoon water
1 Tablespoon butter
2 Tablespoons heavy cream

Instructions

Chop cauliflower into small pieces and add to a large casserole dish.

Add 1 Tablespoon water, cover, and microwave on high for 5 minutes.

Remove and let stand for 5 minute.

Drain water from cauliflower and place in a food processor.

Add butter and heavy cream.

Process until smooth.

Scoop out and place in a serving bowl.

Simplistic Green Beans

Description

Sometimes the best things in life are amazingly simple. Take this green bean dish, for example. Only two ingredients deliver taste and fulfillment, complimenting any main dish.

Yields: 4 Servings

Ingredients

1 pound fresh green beans
1 onion, cut in half and sliced thick
1 Tablespoon oil
2 Tablespoons butter
Unrefined sea salt and pepper to taste

Instructions

Using a heavy skillet, sauté green beans, over medium heat, in oil and 1 Tablespoon of butter.

Add onion pieces and continue sautéing until the onions brown.

Turn into a serving bowl and let guests season, to their liking, with salt and pepper.

Dressy Cauliflower Casserole

Description

Cauliflower is a great food for keeping carbs low, but can become quite boring when prepared over and over again. This recipe dresses up this vegetable by using other seasonings for a flavor that almost makes you forget about the main ingredient.

Yields: 6 Servings

Ingredients

1 fresh head cauliflower, broken up, or 1 16 ounce frozen bag, cooked and drained
½ cup onion, diced
1 ½ cup fresh mushrooms
2 Tablespoons butter
¼ cup heavy cream
¼ cup mayonnaise
4 ounces shredded cheddar cheese
¼ cup green onions, chopped

Instructions

Warm oven to 350 degrees F.

Place prepared cauliflower in a greased 2-quart casserole dish.

In a skillet, sauté onion and mushrooms in the butter.

Add to the cauliflower and mix.

Mix in cheese.

In a small bowl, combine cream and mayonnaise.

Pour the sauce over the cauliflower mix and coat well.

Sprinkle the top with green onions.

Bake, covered, for 25 minutes.

Remove lid and bake another 10 minutes, or until the top is brown and crispy.

Chapter 5: Fulfillment with Drinks

Pina Colada Smoothie

Description

Soft drinks and some fruit drinks can be loaded with sugar. By side-stepping this calorie boosting substance, drinks take on a more lasting flavor, keep you from tiring and give your body the liquids that they need.

Yields: 2 Servings

Ingredients

1/2 cup unsweetened coconut milk
1/4 cup plain yogurt
1/2 cup fresh pineapple chunks
1/4 teaspoon coconut extract
1 teaspoon fresh lime juice
8 ice cubes
2 packets sugar substitute
2 lime slices

Instructions

1. In a blender, add all ingredients (except lime slices).

2. Blend on high until smooth.

Add a slice of lime to the edge of each glass to add a zesty twist.

Refreshing Fruit Shake

Description

Shakes do not have to weigh you down with unhealthy calories and leaving you feel sluggish. Try this homemade version of a strawberry milkshake and forget the tired feeling. Double the recipe to share with a friend.

Yields: 1 Serving

Ingredients

1 cup strawberries
1 cup almond flavored low-fat milk
1 packet sugar substitute
1 cube tofu
1 cup ice cubes

Instructions

1. Blend together strawberries, milk, sugar substitute, and tofu in a blender.

2. Add ice cubes and blend again.

Awesome Juice Spritzer

Description

Keeping the kids (and adults) away from soft drinks can be a never ending chore. Keep a 2-liter bottle of refreshing juice spritzer in the frig and no one will even miss the pop.

Yields: 6 Servings

Ingredients

9 ounces pineapple, orange, or pomegranate juice
48 ounces club soda or sparkling water

Instructions

1. Add juice to club soda or sparkling water, using a 2 liter air tight bottle.

Freshly processed and strained fruit can also be used in the place of juice.

Honey Dew Smoothie

Description

Add variety to your beverages by using a little thought of ingredient. The flavor will bring a new twist to boring fruit juices. Light and healthy, this drink only has 110 calories per serving. Increase ingredients to share with family and friends.

Yields: 2 Servings

Ingredients

4 cups cubed honey dew
2 apples, peeled, cored and cubed
2 kiwi fruits, peeled and sliced
3 packets sugar substitute
2 Tablespoons lemon juice
2 cups ice cubes

Instructions

1. Combine all ingredients (except ice cubes) in a blender and blend well.

2. Add ice cubes and blend until ice becomes broken into small pieces.

Apricot Peach Slush

Description

This fruity drink has become a favorite of diabetics because of the sweet flavor and smooth texture. It's hard to think that something so refreshing can be good for you, but it is. Keep plenty of apricot nectar on hand because this beverage will go fast.

Yields: 6 Servings

Ingredients

15 ½ ounces apricot nectar, chilled
2 fresh peaches, peeled, pitted and sliced
1 ½ cups crushed ice
1 Tablespoon lemon juice
1 ½ cups chilled carbonated water

Instructions

1. In a blender, combine the apricot nectar, peaches, lemon juice and crushed ice.

2. Blend until smooth.

3. Spoon into a tall glass, filling halfway.

4. Fill the glass to the top with carbonated water.

Smooth Strawberry Passion

Description

Forget the milkshakes and all the calories and instead, make up a batch of Smooth Strawberry Passion drinks. Low in carbs and fat, this drink is great for a gathering or just to sit on the porch on a hot summer day.

Yields: 6 Servings

Ingredients

4 cups fresh strawberries, sliced
1 banana
1 kiwi fruit
16 ounces vanilla yogurt
1 cup ice cubes

Instructions

Using a blender, add strawberries, banana, and yogurt.

Blend until creamy.

Add ice cubes, one at a time, blending until they are broken up.

Pour in glasses, garnishing with kiwi fruit.

Wean Off of Soft Drinks

In a world of perfection, you would cut out all soda. The sugary sweeteners, found in soda, is almost impossible to break down. However, the addiction to soft drinks can cause you to abandon a new eating plan, after a day or two. If you currently have sugary soda in your daily life, definitely change to a diet brand - but don't try to cut it out cold turkey. You want to succeed in your new diet, so it is okay to start out slow. Slowly wean yourself off of the addictive, artificial taste by trading for a more refreshing taste of natural ingredients.

Chapter 6: Make Ahead Snacks

Sweet Popcorn Extravaganza

Description

Showtime in front of the TV will become even more exciting when there is a big bowl of crunchy, sweet snacks ready for each turn. Make this light and wholesome finger food ahead of time and keep in an air tight container.

Yields: 8 Servings

Ingredients

4 Tablespoons butter, melted
2 egg whites
2 packets sugar substitute
½ teaspoon vanilla extract
½ teaspoon cinnamon
¼ teaspoon salt
1 ½ cups low-carb cereal flakes
3 ounces pecans or almonds
4 cups pop corn

Instructions

1. Heat oven to 300 degrees F.

2. Lay a sheet of aluminum foil over a baking sheet and spray with Canola oil.

3. In a small bowl, combine butter, egg whites, sugar substitute, vanilla, cinnamon and salt.

4. Whisk the egg mixture until well blended.

5. Using a large bowl, add cereal and nuts and coat with the melted butter.

6. Add popcorn and lightly toss.

7. Pour mixture onto the baking sheet and spread evenly.

8. Bake for 20 to 25 minutes, or until crispy.

9. Remove and cool.

Store in an air tight container until show time. By adding the popcorn to the mixture last, there will be less clumps for hands to grab.

Granola Mini Balls

Description

These little bundles are the perfect size for snacking or grabbing as a quick energy picker-upper. Leave a plateful on the table and the refrigerator door will have less activity.

Yields: 6 Servings

Ingredients

2 cups granola
½ cup raisins
½ cup pecans, chopped
½ cup dried apricots
1 cup low-fat dried milk
1 cup creamy peanut butter
1/3 cup honey

Instructions

1. In a large bowl, mix granola, raisins, pecans, apricots, dried milk, and honey.

2. Gradually add peanut butter, stirring until all ingredients are well covered.

3. Using your hands, form into small balls and place on small squares of waxed paper.

4. Place the balls, including the waxed paper on a serving plate. The waxed paper will keep the balls from sticking to one another.

Homemade Sweet Granola Mix

Description

Teach your kids how to have a great snack by letting them help make this sweet, crunchy treat. They will learn how to eat healthier, plus have something to munch on while playing video games.

Yields: 8 Servings

Ingredients

1 cup rolled oats
1 cup almonds
1 cup unsalted peanuts
1 cup raw sunflower seeds
1 cup flax seeds
1 cup sweetened coconut flakes
1 cup dried cranberries
3 Tablespoons brown sugar syrup

Instructions

1. Preheat oven to 250 degrees F.

2. Line a baking sheet with parchment sheets.

3. Use a large mixing bowl and add all ingredients.

4. Mix well with a wooden spoon or spatula.

5. Spread onto the baking sheet and flatten.

6. Bake for 15 minutes.

7. Remove and break up the granola pieces.

8. Bake for an additional 15 minutes.

9. Remove and cool.

10. Place into an airtight container.

Healthy Workout Granola Mix

Description

Here is another type of granola treat that is favored by athletes after a good workout. However, it was soon found to be a favorite of youngsters, as well.

Yields: 8 servings

Ingredients

1 cup rolled oats
1 cup almonds
1 cup dried cranberries
1 ½ cups butter
½ cup brown sugar
2 Tablespoons honey
½ teaspoon vanilla extract

Instructions

1. Preheat oven to 375 degrees F.

2. Coat baking tray with spray canola oil
3. In a large bowl, combine the oats, almonds, dried cranberries, and ground cinnamon.

4. Blend well with a large wooden spoon or spatula.

5. Add the butter, brown sugar, honey and vanilla extract together in a separate bowl, blending well.

6. Pour the butter mixture into the dry ingredients and mix until all is coated.

7. Spread the mixture onto the greased baking tray and press down to flatten.

8. Place in the oven for 20 to 25 minutes.

9. Remove and cool.

10. Either cut into bars, or break up the pieces for a bite size treat.

Low-Carb Nachos and Fixings

Description

Many people admit that their toughest part of staying on a low-carb diet, is giving up chips. Here is a unique way to have it all. Chips, cheese, salsa, at an amazing 6.5 net carbs. The secret is in the chips and here is a way to have your cake and eat it, too.

Yields: 10 Servings

Ingredients

8 ounces low-carb soy chips
1 cup chopped black olives
4 ½ ounces chopped, mild green chilies
12 ounces cheddar cheese, grated
2/3 cup sour cream
2/3 cup salsa

Instructions

1. Move rack in oven to within 6 inches of the broiler and preheat to broil.

2. Line 2 baking sheets with aluminum foil and spray lightly, with canola oil spray.

3. Arrange the soy chips on the baking sheets in a single layer.

4. Top each chip with olives and chilies.

5. Sprinkle with cheese.

6. Place in oven and broil for 45 to 60 seconds.

7. Remove and transfer to a platter.

8. Place sour cream in one small bowl and the salsa in another.

9. Serve together.

Crispy Fried Fish with Lemon Sauce

Description

Who says you can't have fried fish on a low-carb diet? Choose pollock, whiting, haddock or scrod, and don't forget the sauce.

Yields: 4 Servings

Ingredients

4 8-ounce fish fillets
1 egg
2 ounces baked potato chips, ground
2 Tablespoons water
2 Tablespoons canola oil
½ cup mayonnaise
3 Tablespoons fresh dill, chopped
2 teaspoons lemon zest, grated
¼ teaspoon pepper

Instructions

1. Spread chip crumbs on a flat surface lined with waxed paper.

2. In a wide bowl, whisk 1 egg with water and brush on each fillet.

3. Heat a non-stick skillet to medium heat and add 1 Tablespoon canola oil

4. Dredge each fillet through the crumbs and place in the hot skillet.

5. Turn each fillet once after cooking about 3 to 4 minutes, or until golden brown.

6. Gently remove to plates
7. In a small bowl, mix the mayonnaise, dill, zest and pepper for dip.

Chapter 7: Let's Have a Picnic

Oriental Cabbage Salad

Description

Summer comes with lots of potlucks and bar-b-ques. Trying to watch your eating habits can be very trying with hamburgers and hot dogs being served. Start bringing great side dishes to get togethers and introduce the crowd to great tasting foods.

Yields: 4 Servings

Ingredients

½ head grated, green cabbage
3 chopped scallions
2 Tablespoons sesame oil
2 Tablespoons rice wine vinegar
2 Tablespoons toasted sesame seeds

Instructions

1. In a large serving bowl, combine the cabbage, scallions, oil and vinegar.

2. Toss well, then refrigerate.

3. Right before serving, add the sesame seeds and toss lightly.

Kickin' Deviled Eggs

Description

Deviled eggs are an all-time favorite at picnics, but these beauties will make the crowd stop and say, WOW! The special ingredient may surprise you, and certainly, anyone who indulges. With 1 gram of carbs and 178 calories, maybe it won't hurt to have a couple.

Yields: 20 eggs

Ingredients

10 large eggs
4 Tablespoons cream cheese
½ cup mayonnaise
2 Tablespoons fresh chives, minced
2 teaspoons wasabi paste
pepper
1 teaspoon sea salt

Instructions

1. Boil eggs in a single layer, using a large saucepan, for 7 minutes.

2. Turn off heat and cover saucepan for 15 minutes.

3. Drain water off and refill with cold water. Let stand for at least 10 minutes.

4. Peel eggs and cut in half, long way.

5. Remove yolks and place in a large bowl.

6. Add the cream cheese and wasabi paste.

7. Mash with a fork or masher until everything is blended and resembles small crumbs.

8. Stir in the mayonnaise and chives and add pepper to taste.

9. Place the yolk mixture in a pastry bag and squeeze filling into the white cups of the eggs.

10. Make a swirling motion, beginning with the outer layer and working to a point in the middle.

11. Just before serving, sprinkle with sea salt.

Chicken Waldorf Salad

Description

Everyone loves the flavor of apples and walnuts, mixed with greens and a tart dressing. Make it a meal by adding chicken and using a new kind of dressing that will make guests request, time and time again.

Yields: 4 Servings

Ingredients

4 cooked and cubed chicken breasts
1 cup chopped celery
1 ½ cup chopped apples
4 ounces walnut pieces
4 Tablespoons raisins
1 cup low-fat Italian dressing
10 cups Iceberg and Bibb lettuce

Instructions

1. Place the lettuce, chicken, apples and celery in a large serving bowl and toss well.

2. Pour the Italian dressing over all and toss to coat.

3. Add the walnut pieces and raisins, gently blending.

Fresh Green Bean and Tomato Italiano

Description

There is nothing more flavorful than the taste of fresh green beans that are served up steamed and crunchy. Bring this dish to your outdoor party and you will find that even the youngsters will be tempted with their presence. This is a quick and easy side dish that delivers a compliment to any type of meat.

Yields: 6 Servings

Ingredients

3 cups fresh green beans
2 plum tomatoes, sliced into thin wedges
2 Tablespoons fresh basil
¼ cup Italian dressing

Instructions

1. Steam green beans for 10 minutes, just long enough to remove the raw texture.

2. Cool and add tomatoes and basil.

3. Pour dressing over all and toss lightly, just to coat.

Confetti Pasta Salad

Description

Here is a dish that is almost too beautiful to eat. Colorful and robust, it will seem more like a main dish than a complimentary side. Increase the size to share for an outdoor BBQ or other picnic event.

Yields: 4 Servings

Ingredients

1 cup multicolored, low-carb penne, cooked
4 artichoke hearts, diced
4 ounces thinly sliced turkey breast strips
8 ounces fresh mozzarella, diced
4 Tablespoon red pepper
8 Tablespoons fresh, chopped green beans
4 Tablespoons olive oil
4 teaspoons balsamic vinegar
2 teaspoons fresh oregano, chopped

Instructions

1. Combine pasta, artichoke hearts, turkey, mozzarella, red pepper and green beans in a large salad bowl.

2. In a small bowl, mix oil, vinegar, and oregano.

3. Pour over the pasta mixture and toss.

Cobb Salad with Crab

Description

Seafood is the main ingredient that gives this salad a wonderful flavor. Along with other cobb salad favorite additions, this side dish goes very well with those lake-caught fish.

Yields: 4 Servings

Ingredients

12 cups romaine lettuce, torn into bite-size pieces
12 ounce cooked crab meat
2 cups cherry tomatoes, halved
1 cup crumbled blue cheese
½ cup olive oil raspberry flavored dressing

Instructions

1. In a large serving bowl, add lettuce, crab meat, tomatoes and blue cheese.

2. Toss well then add dressing and toss again.

Chapter 8: Exciting Desserts

Chocolate Sponge Cake with Strawberries

Description

There is something wrong with a low-carb diet that does not allow for the sweet pleasures in life, mainly cake and chocolate. This dessert will satisfy both with rich flavor and texture.

Yields: 10 Servings

Ingredients

7 egg whites
1/8 tsp cream of tartar
¾ cup sugar
3 egg yolks
1 teaspoon vanilla
1 cup cake flour
3 Tablespoons melted butter
1 ½ ounces semisweet chocolate
2 Tablespoons canola oil
12 plump strawberries

Instructions

1. Heat oven to 350 degr F.

2. Use a large bowl to beat the egg whites and cream of tartar until foamy.

3. Add the sugar, gradually, while whipping into a meringue, with soft peaks.

4. In another bowl, beat together the egg yolks and vanilla.

5. Add the egg yolk mixture to the egg whites, gradually, folding until well blended.

6. Fold in the flour, stirring until all has been absorbed.

7. Pour batter into the cake batter and fold gently.

9. Spoon the batter into a 10-inch tube pan and bake for 35-40 minutes, or until the center proves clean, with a tooth pick.

10. Remove the cake and turn upside down on a large bottle so all sides are exposed to the air.

11. Cool for about an hour.

12. Remove the pan and run a knife along the sides of the pan to loosen the cake, then invert onto a wire rack to further cool.

13. Place on a serving dish.

14. Melt the chocolate and oil, slowly to keep from scorching and drizzle over the cooled cake.

15. Dot the top with strawberries.

Luscious Lime Cheesecake Tarts

Description

Cheesecake can add the final touch to a great meal, or be a special treat for friends that visit. Adding the tartness of lime and the sweetness of kiwi, will let you savor every bite.

Yields: 12 Servings

Ingredients

12 vanilla wafers
¾ cup cottage cheese
8 ounces low-fat cream cheese
¼ cup sugar or sugar substitute
2 eggs
1 Tablespoon grated lime rind
1 Tablespoon fresh lime juice
1 teaspoon vanilla
¼ cup vanilla flavored yogurt
2 kiwis, peeled, sliced and halved

Instructions

1. Using a 12-cup muffin pan, line each cup with a paper muffin liner.

2. Heat oven to 350 degrees F.

3. Place a vanilla wafer in the bottom of each cup.

4. Using a blender, add the cottage cheese, cream cheese and sugar. Blend well.

5. Add the eggs, lime rind, lime juice and vanilla. Beat until smooth.

6. Spoon the mixture into the lined muffin cups and bake for 15-20 minutes, or until well set.

7. Remove from oven and chill completely.

8. Right before serving, spread the vanilla flavored yogurt on top and garnish with kiwi pieces.

Fruity Bread Pudding

Description

Bread pudding can become a sinful dish when laced with peaches and cream. Serve up this delightful dessert to family and friends. Have the recipe ready to share because everyone will want to know your secret ingredients.

Yields: 12 Servings

Ingredients

1 teaspoon butter, softened
6 slices low-carb bread, cubed
1 ½ cups fresh or frozen chopped peaches
4 eggs
1 cup heavy cream
½ cup sugar
¼ teaspoon nutmeg
1 ½ teaspoons vanilla
2 Tablespoons sliced almonds

Instructions

1. Warm oven to 350 F degrees.

2. Butter an 8-inch square baking dish
3. Add bread crumbs and peaches to dish and toss.

4. In a medium-sized bowl, add eggs, cream, sugar, nutmeg and vanilla, and whisk together.

5. Pour the egg mixture over the bread and peaches.

6. Let stand for 10 minutes to allow the bread to absorb the liquid mixture.

7. Sprinkle almonds on top of the dish.

8. Place the dish inside a 9x11 pan, filled with boiling water. The water should rise halfway up the sides of the 8-inch dish.

9. Bake for 45 to 50 minutes, or until a clean knife shows that it is done.

Almond Ricotta Pudding

Description

Take a break with a smooth, luscious pudding that is satisfying and only 8 carbs per serving. Quick to make, this recipe is designed for 1 serving but can be stretched to include the whole family.

Yields: 1 Serving

Ingredients

½ cup ricotta cheese
¼ teaspoon almond extract
1 packet sweetener
1 teaspoon slivered toasted almonds

Instructions

1. Mix the ricotta cheese, almond extract and sugar substitute.

2. Sprinkle with almonds.

Enjoy.

Heavenly Chocolate Sorbet

Description

Remember the fudge ice pops that you enjoyed as a child? Here is an adult version that will bring back memories, yet satisfy the grown up you. You will need an ice-cream maker for this recipe. This treat is not for kids, the more reason to sneak away and enjoy.

Yields: 4 Servings

Ingredients

2 cups ice cold water
1 teaspoon unflavored gelatin
1 ½ cups sugar-free chocolate syrup
1 cup low-fat milk
3 Tablespoons dark rum

Instructions

1. Add 2 Tablespoons ice water in a glass measuring cup.

2. Sprinkle with gelatin.

3. Microwave for 20 seconds to dissolve the gelatin.

3. In a medium-sized bowl, add ¾ cup syrup, the remaining ice water, milk and rum.

4. Stir until blended.

5. Add the remaining chocolate syrup into the mix and whisk.

6. Add the dissolved gelatin and stir.

7. Pour the mixture into an ice-cream maker and churn, according to instructions.

8. Remove and place in an airtight container and place in the freezer until ready to serve.

Non Traditional Squash Pie

Description

Pumpkin pie may be the tradition, but there's a new version in town. Serve up this wonderful dessert that offers much lower calories and carbs and start a new traditional during the holidays, or any time.

Yields: 8 Servings

Ingredients

3 cups cooked winter squash, mashed
¾ cup unsweetened coconut milk
¼ cup honey
3 eggs
2 teaspoons pumpkin pie spice
1 ½ teaspoons maple extract
1 ½ Tablespoons arrowroot powder
1 ¼ teaspoons unrefined sea salt, finely ground
½ teaspoon sugar

Instructions

1. Warm oven to 350 degr F.

2. Mix all ingredients with a mixer or in a food processor. If the consistency is too thick, add a little water, 1 teaspoon each, until no longer stiff.

3. Pour into a greased 10-inch pie pan and bake for 50 to 60 minutes, or until a knife comes out clean, when placed in the center.

4. Allow pie to cool then chill for another 30 minutes, to firm.

Chapter 9: Wise Wok Cooking

Shrimp Egg Rolls

Description

Reintroduce your wok to keep fat and sugar limited. It may take some time to prepare these awesome egg rolls, but the results are well worth the trouble.

Yields: 8 Servings

Ingredients

½ pounds raw shrimp, cleaned and deveined
1 teaspoon sherry
1 teaspoon salt
½ teaspoon cornstarch
3 Tablespoons canola oil
3 cups diced celery
½ teaspoon sugar
1 Tablespoon water
½ cup fresh bean sprouts
1 cup shredded lettuce
1 cup chopped water chestnuts
16 egg-roll wrappers

Instructions

1. In a small bowl, combine shrimp, sherry, salt and cornstarch.

2. Let the mixture marinate for 12 to minutes.

3. Heat 1 tablespoon oil in work.

4. Add shrimp mixture and stir-fry until shrimp is pink and firm.

5. Remove to a mixing bowl.

6. Add remaining oil to wok and add celery, stir-frying for 2 to 3 minutes.

7. Add sugar and water.

8. Cover and let steam for 1 minute.

9. Remove cover and stir-fry until all the liquid has evaporated.

10. Add to shrimp mixture.

11. Add remaining ingredients.

12. Blend well.

13. Prepare wrappers by laying out flat.

14. Fill each one with ¼ cup shrimp mixture.

15. Lift lower triangle of wrapper over filling and tuck the point under.

16. Leave the upper point of the wrapper flat.

17. Bring the 2 end flaps up and over the enclosed filling and press flaps down firmly.

18. Brush cold water over the exposed triangles and roll the filled portion until you have a neat package. The water will seal your ingredients protectively.

19. Repeat until you have 16 filled egg rolls.

20. Fill the wok with 3 inches of oil in the center.

21. Heat to 375 degrees F.

22. Using tongs, lower 4 eggs rolls into the oil and deep fry for 3 to 4 minutes, or until golden brown.

23. Drain on paper towels, blotting out all of the oil.

24. Repeat until all egg rolls have been cooked.

Serve with hot mustard, plum sauce or soy sauce. You can also store for later use by cooling and wrapping in plastic wrap, then placing in freezer bags to refrigerate or freeze.

Mandarin Cauliflower and Broccoli Medley

Description

Making your vegetables more interesting, will create a reason for your family to try any new variation. The aroma of this mixture, while stir-frying, will have everyone sitting at the table, ready to enjoy.

Yields: 4 Servings

Ingredients
2 Tablespoons canola oil
½ teaspoon salt
10 mushrooms, sliced lengthwise
1 small onion, minced
1 cup water
1 ½ cups bite-size cauliflower pieces
1 ½ cups bite-size broccoli pieces
½ cup water
2 teaspoons sugar
2 teaspoons cornstarch dissolved in 1 Tablespoon water

Instructions

1. Heat oil and salt in wok.

2. Add mushrooms and onion.

3. Stir-fry for 2 minutes or until tender.

4. Add water and bring to a boil.

5. Cover and steam for 5 minutes.

6. Uncover and add broccoli.

7. Cover and steam for an additional 10 minutes, stirring occasionally.

8. Uncover and add remaining water and sugar.

9. Bring to a simmer and add cornstarch mix.

10. Stir until sauce thickens and all vegetables are well coated.

Stir Fry Chicken and Peaches

Description

A delicate sauce make this stir fry chicken recipe a hit with the family. Low-cal and nutritious, peaches all extra flavor to a classic sweet and sour classic dish.

Yields: 6 to 8 Servings

Ingredients
1 3-pound chicken, cut into 8 pieces
1 teaspoon salt
½ teaspoon poultry seasoning
3 Tablespoons cornstarch
1 cup canola oil plus 1 Tablespoon oil
1 clove garlic, peeled and crushed
8 ounces frozen sliced, unsweetened peaches, thawed
1 Tablespoon sugar
2 Tablespoons lemon juice
½ cup chicken broth
2 teaspoons cornstarch dissolved in 1 Tablespoon water
10 ounces frozen snow peas
3 cups hot cooked rice

Instructions

1. Fill wok half full with water.

2. Place chicken pieces in a shallow baking dish and sprinkle with salt and poultry seasoning.

3. Place dish on a wire rack atop the wok and cover.

4. Cover chicken and turn wok on medium-high.

5. Steam the chicken for 45 minutes.

6. Remove and dry chicken pieces.

7. Rub cornstarch into each chicken piece.

8. Remove water from wok and wipe dry.

9. Add 1 cup canola oil into wok and heat to just under sizzling.

10. Fry chicken pieces in the hot oil, 2 or 3 pieces at a time until lightly browned.

11. Remove to a plate, lined with paper towels.

12. Pour oil out of wok and discard.

13. Add 1 Tablespoon oil to wok, add garlic, and stir-fry until brown.

14. Remove and discard garlic.

15. Add peaches and sugar, snow peas, stirring into the garlic liquid.

16. Stir in lemon juice.

17. Add chicken broth and heat to boiling.

18. Stir in dissolved cornstarch.

19. Add snow peas, stirring into the liquid.

20. Cover and steam for 30 seconds.

21. Add chicken pieces to wok and cover.

22. Steam for 30 seconds or until chicken is heated.

Serve over hot cooked rice.

Oriental Rice

Description

It seems that every time you have a Chinese-type of meal, there is tons of white rice left over. Put it to good use with this tasty oriental rice recipe. It will make a great side dish for a lunch or dinner menu Yields: 4 to 6 Serving

Ingredients
1 Tablespoon oil
2 cups cold cooked rice
½ cup chopped water chestnuts
½ cup raisins
¼ cup soy sauce

Instructions

1. Heat oil in wok.

2. Add rice and cook, stirring until coated with oil.

3. Add water chestnuts and raisins.

4. Stir-fry until all is heated.

5. Add soy sauce and blend well.

6. Turn into a serving bowl.

Small portions of leftover meat can also be used for additional flavor.

Sweet and Sour Shrimp

Description

Who doesn't love the awesome flavor of sweet and sour sauce, mixed with shrimp and fresh vegetables. Here is a recipe that will amaze your taste buds and satisfy your hunger.

Yields: 4 Servings

Ingredients
1 carrot, peeled and diagonally sliced
1 green pepper, cut into 1-inch squares
2 cups canola oil
½ teaspoon salt
8 ounces breaded, frozen shrimp
1 clove garlic, peeled and flattened
1 cup unsweetened pineapple chunks, drained (save the juice)
¾ cup mixed sweet pickles, drained

Sauce Ingredients
1 ¼ cup unsweetened pineapple juice
¼ cup white wine vinegar
1 Tablespoon soy sauce
1/3 cup brown sugar
1/4 cup catsup
2 Tablespoons cornstarch

Instructions

Prepare the Sweet and Sour Sauce first.

1. In a small saucepan, combine 1 cup pineapple juice, vinegar, soy sauce, sugar and catsup.

2. Stir over medium heat until simmering.

3. Dissolve cornstarch in ¼ cup pineapple juice and add to pan.

4. Stir until smooth.

5. Remove from heat and set aside.

Stir-Fry Section
1. Place carrot slices in saucepan and cover with water.

2. Boil for 5 minutes
3. Add green pepper and boil for another 5 minutes.

4. Drain and set aside.

5. Add oil and salt to wok.

6. Heat to 375 degrees F.

7. Fry the frozen shrimp, a few at a time, until lightly browned.

8. Drain on paper towels.

9. Remove oil from wok and wipe clean with paper towels.

10. Discard oil.

11. Add 1 Tablespoon oil to wok.

12. Set to high heat.

13. Add garlic, rubbing against sides and bottom until lightly browned.

14. Remove and discard.

15. Add peppers and carrots.

16. Stir-fry for 30 seconds.

17. Add the sweet and sour sauce.

18. Next, add the pineapple chunks and pickles.

19. Stir-fry until hot.

20. Add cooked shrimp and cover all with sauce.

21. Spoon over hot cooked rice.

Pears Cardinal

Description

No one will find these pears boring with the succulent flavor of raspberries, surrounding them. Easy to make while you have your wok out, or use your stove top. Attractive, rich and melt-in-your mouth consistency, make this dessert a great finish to any meal.

Yields: 8 to 10 Servings

Ingredients
6 ripe pears
Red food coloring
20 ounces frozen raspberries, thawed (or fresh is even better)
2 Tablespoons sugar
2 teaspoons cornstarch, dissolved in 2 Tablespoons water
¼ cup kirsch liqueur, or raspberry flavored syrup

Instructions

1. Place a rack in wok that is filled with simmering water.

2. Stand up pears on the rack and cover.

3. Steam for 10 to 15 minutes.

4. Remove pears from rack.

5. Run under cold water to gently remove skin.

6. Rub each pear with a little red food coloring for a blushed appearance.

7. Refrigerate until chilled.

8. Blend raspberries in a blender.

9. Strain out seeds.

10. Place the raspberry puree in a saucepan and bring to a boil.

11. Stir in sugar and dissolved cornstarch.

12. Keep stirring until mixture thickens.

13. Remove from heat and add liqueur or flavored syrup.

14. Refrigerate until well chilled.

15. When ready to serve, place on pear in a serving dish and spoon the sauce over the top.

Chapter 10: List of Low-Carb Foods

Trying to keep all of the terms straight, like carbohydrates, calories, low-fat, and induction, can be difficult to understand. Not all low-carb foods are low-fat, or low in calories. Start with this list of foods that can keep anyone on the straight and narrow in beginning a low-carb diet. After a while, you will learn, just by tasting, how some foods dull your palate in enjoying the rich flavor of natural foods. One of these is sugar. It is a known fact that refined sugar decreases your ability to savor flavor. By ridding your diet of refined sugar, bleached white flour, margarine, and other processed, synthetic additives, you will begin to enjoy the wholesome flavor that low-carb natural foods have to offer.

Cucumbers
Broccoli
Iceberg Lettuce
Celery
White Mushrooms
Turnips
Radishes
Romaine Lettuce
Asparagus
Green Pepper
Okra
Cauliflower
Cabbage
Red Bell Pepper
Spinach
Beets
Green Beans
Carrots
Kale
Sugar Snap Peas
Corn
Onions
Watermelon
Strawberries
Cantaloupe
Avocado

Blackberries
Honeydew Melon
Grapefruit
Oranges
Peaches
Papaya
Cranberries
Plums
Raspberries
Pineapple
Nectarine
Blueberries
Apples
Pears
Kiwi Fruit
Cherries
Tangerines
Mango

If you feel that you just can't stay away from refined sugar, try these natural alternatives in cooking and see how quickly your habit begins to fade.

Molasses
Sorghum
Real Maple Syrup
Maple Sugar
Sucanat or Rapadura
Agave Syrup
Coconut Sugar
Honey

Bread is a real obstacle for many that have grown up on products made from white flour. If you are able to find bread products with any of the following main ingredients, you will be doing your body a favor.

Corn
Soybeans
Oat Bran
Barley
Organic Sprouted Wheat

Millet

Pasta has grown popular in making quick meals but the ingredients can be full of carbs. While many companies are slow to transform a popular-selling product into one that offers good nutrition, one company is gaining ground because of the low-carb content. Known as Shirataki, the starch is made from the root of devil's tongue, a type of yam. While you will probably never find this product in your local grocery store, keep your eyes open for new types of pasta alternatives in the foreign cuisine section.

Chapter 11: Tips for Prepping

People raised in countries, outside of the United States, are constantly amazed at how our grocery shopping is done. They are used to shopping for fresh produce and seafood on a daily basis, not weekly, as is practiced in the states. How can anything be fresh when it is allowed to set for a week?

To say that it is simple to eat healthier on a low carb diet, according to American standards, would be misleading. Manufacturers of ready-made food stuffs , count on the fact that there is too little time to spend on healthy eating. Popping a cardboard box into the microwave or opening a can, has replaced wholesome foods with convenience. Unfortunately, this way of thinking has led us to where we are today. Weight gain, inadequate vitamin supply, and slow metabolism, is the result of pumping your body with preservatives and sugars that prevent a healthy system. While time is on everyone's mind, there are some short cuts that you can take to prepare for low carb meals.

Freeze, Freeze, Freeze

In the summer, fresh vegetables are everywhere. But when winter sets in, finding produce can make your search for fresh foods, a real chore. This year, snap up those great looking veggies and freeze so you will have plenty on hand during the winter months.

Not all vegetables freeze well. Those with a high water content can become mushy and less flavorful, like onions and cucumbers. But many other types can retain their shape, presence and vitamins, for meal prepping. Here are some examples of vegetables that can be frozen and ready to use:

Asparagus
Beans

Broccoli
Cauliflower
Squash and Zucchini
Eggplant
Snow Peas

How to Properly Freeze:

It is not difficult to prepare vegetables for future use, but it does take a little bit of planning. Pick a day for putting up your family's favorite veggies and follow these simple instructions to make an ample supply.

Supplies needed:

3-quart Saucepan
Wire Basket
Jelly roll pan
Waxed paper
Freezer Bags
Marking Pen

Instructions for Blanching

Select your veggies and prepare by cleaning, cutting and making meal ready.

Fill the saucepan half full of water and bring to a boil.

Put the prepared veggies into the wire basket and plunge into the boiling water for 3 minutes.

Remove and drain. Pat dry to remove any excess water.

Line the jelly roll pan with waxed paper and lay out your vegetables in single file.

Place the jelly roll pan in the freezer, just long enough for the food to freeze.

Remove and place in freezer bags, squeezing out as much excess water, as possible.

Mark and date each bag and return to the freezer.

By getting into the habit of preparing garden fresh vegetables for future use, you can rest assured that your family will receive no preservatives or additives from packaged foods.

10 Tips for Staying on a Low-Cal Plan

No one claims that it is easy to break bad habits, but if you look at where you are, and where you want to be, anything is possible. Remember when you thought that using a cell phone was the most impossible thing you had ever done? But now you probably wonder how you ever lived without it. Everyone dislikes change but when the future turns out for the better, you wonder how you ever thought differently. Try some of these tips and you will soon be forgetting about those bad eating habits.

1. Use coconut as a sweetener. Why is coconut downplayed so much? It is a wonderful, sweet and tasty type of low-carb accessory that can become irreplaceable. Use it in main dish recipes, savor the juice and discover that it is very addicting.

2. Who started the rumor that eggs were bad? Eggs are a great source of protein and can be eaten alone or used in salads and meals. They are also very portable for a quick energy boost. Use to make sauces, to add texture to foods, or just as a snack in the middle of the day.

3. Never throw leftovers away. You just spent a lot of time on a low-cal meal for your family and believe it or not, you have some scraps to deal with. You already know how good they are for you so wrap them up and use on a salad for lunch tomorrow.

4. Herbs are better than salt. We all have the habit of salting everything that is set in front of us. Break this habit by keeping a variety of herbs close by. The selection will be interesting and fun, plus a lot better than salt, which does nothing but harm your body.

5. Rice is a great filler but not the best when it comes to nutrition. Try something different, like ground cauliflower. The taste will not be so ho-hum and you might just trick your brain into thinking that it is rice, but somehow, even better.

6. Make good use of your muffin pan. Part of the problem with staying on a low- carb diet menu, is thinking that you are going to starve. The portions seem so tiny and your mind just cannot grab hold of the fact that you will ever be satisfied. Start using a muffin pan to fill with portions so you will get used to having enough. Start with something filling, like pudding or chicken salad. You will be surprised just how much a muffin cup can hold.

7. Salads can be the spice of life. How many other foods are so flexible to accept fruit, meat, and vegetables, without ruining the taste? In addition, dressings and sauces can be an endless supply of flavor. From cheeses to herbs, lemons and limes, you can transform a salad into any flavor you desire.

8. Think of a lettuce leaf as a piece of bread and the need to be fulfilled with a sandwich, will slowly fade away. Wraps are becoming popular with anything and everything. Meat, cheese, pickles, or a mixture of favorite foods. Iceberg lettuce has big meaty leaves for wrapping up tuna salad, eggs, chicken breast, and more.

9. Go on an adventure to an Asian store and look at the labels of pasta. You will probably see some words that are foreign to you, but more than likely, they represent roots and vegetables instead of chemical additives that you do recognize. Asians are not big on bread and grains that make them feel sluggish. Ask someone in the

market about the ingredients, or write down the names and search for yourself.

10. If sweets are your downfall, don't deprive yourself and make the craving worse. Enjoy some chocolate or puddings that can be found on a low carb diet food list. Make ahead to keep on hand for when that craving hits.

Deciding to go on a low-carb diet is not just a choice for losing weight, but changing the way that you look at food. Our society has become accustomed to eating anything that announces 'low-fat' or 'low-carb, that we have been brainwashed into accepting almost anything. Always shop for fresh, or frozen, and learn to enjoy the taste of food that has been replaced with high fat and glucose filled preservatives. Not only will you feel better, but your weight will automatically begin to burn off and give you more energy.

Section 2: Paleolithic Cookbook

The standard western diet may be hurting or killing your body in so many ways, that it can be difficult to keep up with all of the health reports related to unhealthy eating. The Paleolithic diet has been popularly known for many decades, however history seems to show that early human ancestors were living on this "diet" was around 200,000 years ago! Humans were introduced into farming approximately 10,000 years producing a heavy growth grains, bread, pasta, starchy foods and processed foods. However, evidence suggests that evolution is slow to adapt to new types of food that the body may not be used to. This is why the foods including (modern) bread, grease, and processed foods are hard for humans to move on from and onto a healthier lifestyle.

What is Paleo?

The paleo lifestyle tries to follow the diet of those from ancient times of indigenous people and is referred to as the "Paleolithic Diet" as it is from the Stone Age or Paleolithic Age era. The paleolithic diet has additional names it is referred to including, "Stone Age Diet", "Hunter-Gatherer Diet", or the "Cave Man Diet". The Paleolithic diet offers a plethora of health benefits for those who have given it a try. The paleolithic diet isn't another fad diet as it has been a way of eating thousands of years and it is a healthier option for people to take. Anthropologists have found that tribal people who have only been on the paleolithic diet are slimmer, stronger and healthier compared to those who aren't on the diet. These people do not suffer with cavities, dental problems, and have straight teeth. They also have perfect eyesight, rarely battle with arthritis, diabetes, obesity, heart disease, stroke, depression, cancer, and hypertension and schizophrenia disorders. There are approximately 84 tribes of hunter-gatherers left in this world who eat a Paleolithic diet. These people get daily adequate exercise which also helps them to stay healthy too. The tribal people have never evolved further like current civilization has done. The paleolithic diet is an advanced nutritional plan using wild plants and animals of different species. This diet has been around for over 2.5 million years however it ended 10,000 years ago when agriculture was developed. The Paleolithic diet theory introduced dieters with features of holistic and, comprehensive dietary combined together.

Why Go the Paleolithic Route?

The paleolithic diet should provide everything that the body needs to function properly. The primary dietary components are all covered, such as vitamins, phytosterols, proteins, fats, carbohydrates, and antioxidants. This diet is needed as it is programmed within our genes to eat these types of foods and discard foods that do not fit within the paleolithic diet.

Indigenous cultures that are around in this present day still eat the same diet of foods they have eaten for centuries have been considered primitive for not changing their diets. Instead these hunter-gatherers eat the foods that are in their area don't suffer what modern eaters suffer with today. Anthropologists has studied and compared these people with modernized people and they found that the results in association between diet and disease is completely clear that diseases such as diabetes, heart disease, cancer, arthritis and many other diseases were rarely found among the hunter gatherers.

Many dieters found that, after eating Paleo for three weeks:

BMI dropped by about 0.8
Average weight loss was around 5 pounds
Blood pressure fell by an average of three mmHg
Increase in antioxidants
Healthier potassium-sodium balance
Levels of plasminogen activator inhibitor (blood thickening agent) dropped by 72%.

Benefits of the Paleo Lifestyle

The top benefit of the paleolithic diet are eating foods that are naturally high in fiber. Fiber helps to reduce constipation, lower cholesterol, and lowers risks of diabetes and coronary heart disease. The paleolithic diet focuses on helping people lose weight with eating foods that were available during the Paleolithic era. These foods consist of meat, eggs, vegetables, roots, fish, mushrooms and berries. Our bodies are designed to handle foods loaded in high protein, and low carbohydrates however we are not genetically ready to handle low protein and high carb diets during these modern times. Eating a natural diet instead of a diet filled with processed foods, sugar-filled, and grain products.

The paleolithic diet offers the body a higher proportion of fat compared to the average Western diet. This higher proportion gives the body an additional health benefit of providing more energy and helps the body perform better. The fat found in modern diets is primarily unhealthy, consisting of a lot of trans fats. The quality of fat a body needs to consist of fat soluble nutrients including vitamins A, D, E, and K and the CoQ10 (coenzyme) can't be absorbed without the presence of fat. All of these vitamins are very important for the body and avoiding nutrient deficiencies.

Omega-3's provides many benefits for the body such as helping to increase brain size, and forming brain tissue. The omega-3 fatty acids are essential in supporting biochemical processes, creating membranes in cells which keep tissues healthy and maintaining the body's metabolism. It not only improves physical health but also improves mental health, build immune system, cardiovascular strength, and healthy digestion.

Paleo Food Types

Foods to eat

The paleolithic diets come into different types of restrictions depending on the dieter's preferences. The basic paleolithic diet consists of eating foods that are as close to nature or as natural as possible. These foods include:

Meats – lean beef, chuck steak, lean veal, long broil, top sirloin, chicken, fish, pork, seafood, etc.
Other Meat – venison, alligator, bison, reindeer, rabbit, pheasant, wild turkey, wild boar, goal, rattlesnake, emu, caribou, etc.
Vegetables -
Fruits
Nuts & seeds
Seed oils – olive, avocado, palm, coconut, almond, walnut, pecan, macadamia, hazelnut)
Water
Coffee and tea - drink the coffee black or with unsweetened almond milk

Foods to avoid

Grains – barley, oats, rice, wheat, maize, rye, wild rice, millet, corn, etc.
Grain-like Seeds – buckwheat, quinoa, amaranth
Sugar – soft drinks, fruit drinks, candy, honey
Legumes – all beans, lentils, miso, etc
Dairy – butter, cheese, ice cream, milk, yogurt, creamer
Any processed foods

Paleo Confusion

How to know if a food type adheres to the paleo plan.

There are many continuous ongoing debates on whether a certain food type adheres to the paleo plan as the diet focuses on what the first people ate before farming began. However, research is being done to find out if the first people ate potatoes. However, most speculate they did. The confusion comes from certain foods that can't really be classified as Paleo or not, like honey, oats or potato. The truth is, that the paleolithic diet plan isn't completely cut and dry. Saying that, most of the foods listed as paleo provide enough variety and satiety to continue with, without feeling like "cheating".

Paleo Food List

All of the following foods are paleo friendly to eat.

Protein
Eggs
Fish
bass
cod
mackerel
grouper
halibut
herring
red snapper
salmon
Lean Beef and lean cuts
Steaks – flank and chuck
           Lean hamburger beef

Veal
Sirloin

Lean Lamb
lamb chops and loin

Lean Poultry
Chicken, hen and turkey breast

Other Meats
bison – ostrich
elk - squab
alligator - goat
bear - goose
kangaroo - caribou
pheasant - rattlesnake
rabbit –quail
reindeer - emu
turtle – wild turkey
wild boar - venison

Shellfish
crab - clams
abalone - crayfish
lobster – shrimp
scallops - oysters
mussels

Fats
Brazil nuts - almonds
Avocado - coconut
cashews – flaxseed oil
coconut oil
chestnuts

Cold pressed nuts and seeds
walnuts
pecans pumpkin seeds
pistachios
pine nuts
sunflower seeds
sesame seeds

Vegetables
cauliflower - celery
artichoke - asparagus
beet greens
beets - bell pepper
broccoli
Kale - Brussels sprouts
cabbage – carrots - tomato
endive - green onion
Kohlrabi - watercress
collards - cucumber
lettuce - mushroom
mustard greens
onions - parsley
parsnip - peppers
pumpkin - rutabaga
radish - seaweed

spinach - tomatillos
Swiss chard – squash
turnips and turnip greens

Fruits
apple - apricot
banana - blackberry
boysenberry - papaya
cantaloupe - cassava melon
cherimoya - cherries
cranberry - figs
gooseberry - grapefruit
grapes - guava
honeydew -lychee
lemon - lime
kiwi –orange -mango
nectarine -
passion fruit -plums
peaches - pears
persimmon - pineapple
pomegranate - strawberry
raspberry – tangerine
star fruit - watermelon
tangerine
rhubarb

Sample Daily Meal Plan for Beginners

It can be difficult coming up with an original menu plan and easily eat something that is not Paleo related. The best option is to create a menu plan that will help you to make some good food choices and consistently stay on your Paleolithic diet. Create a meal plan that will last for a week or two so if possible purchase at least two weeks worth of food. Keep in mind that it's okay you can skip a meal whenever you want as the Paleolithic diet isn't about eating three meals a day. In this sample menu day plan there are **three** meals and a snack added providing you with enough options to work and play around with it.

Sample Menu Day Plan:

	Breakfast	Lunch	Dinner	Snack
Monday	Berries with coconut milk and mixed nuts	Broccoli and Pine Nut Soup	Meatballs with Crunchy Sweet Potato Chips	Pistachio Salsa
Tuesday	Scrambled Eggs with Mushroom	Cucumber Hot Dogs	Pumpkin and Chicken Curry	Grilled Tomatoes
Wednesday	Salmon and Zucchini Fritters	Roast Vegetables in Orange and Rosemary	Chicken with Macadamia Topping	Nut Butter Cucumber Sandwich
Thursday	Mushroom and Meat Omelet	Dory with Beetroot Salad	Lamb Chops	Tomato Salsa
Friday	Lemon Pancakes	Moroccan Lamb with Squash	Chicken and Egg Salad with Almond Sautéed Sauce	Cashew Nut Dip

Eating Paleo in Day to Day Life

Restaurants and Eating Out

Paleolithic dieters need to find paleo food friendly restaurants and eateries that cater specifically to their diet. There has been a slow trickle of restaurants available catering to natural and raw foods for health conscious people. Avoid leaving your Paleolithic diet up to chance as the failure rates are high when that is done. Instead look into planning ahead by preparing a list of Paleo-friendly restaurants near your home and work. However, keep in mind that your social life is completely different compared to your Paleo ancestors so there will be a trade off of some sort involved. So look into minimizing the damage and try to find more desirable options on the menu and then tighten up on your diet for the next several days. Your ancestors they didn't have temptations all around them to pull them off of their diet however they didn't consider the Paleolithic diet as a diet but as a means of survival.

While out in restaurants, tell the waiter you have a gluten allergy and that includes any grains. Be serious about the topic and they will know to take it seriously and make sure that nothing has touched a non-paleo food or product. Ask for your meal to be cooked with olive oil.

Social Eating

When out with friends do let them know that you won't accept any bad foods. They should know about your diet beforehand so that it will not be a surprise. This is especially important if you dealing with an autoimmune disease or a digestive problem, or are trying to lose weight. Bringing some food of your own will also help to alleviate any issues that may arise. Allow your friends to taste the food you're eating and it will give you an added topic to discuss with your friends.

Food Preparation

Food meal planning helps with knowing what to prepare and eat. The sample meal planner in this book helps in providing ideas and deciding on the best options. Preparing your meals ahead of time instead of cooking daily is a timesaver.

Meal Frequency and Amounts

A person should in general eat when they are hungry, however eating at least 3-4 times a day is a good way to go. It all depends on what you feel fits your overall needs and schedule. The idea on the amount of food to consume meets closer to the FDA's RDI (Recommended Daily Intake) measurements. For protein, individuals on a 2000 calorie diet may need approximately 50% of protein.

Recipe Ideas

Breakfast

Mushroom and Pine Nuts Scrambled Eggs

Ingredients

3 eggs
2 teaspoons of finely chopped onions
2 tablespoons of finely chopped chives
1 cup of slice mushrooms
1 tbsp of oil
1 tablespoon of pine nuts
Salt and pepper

Instructions

Place the oil in the frying pan on medium heat and fry the onions for at least 3-4 minutes until they are browned lightly then remove the mushrooms from the pan.

In a bowl whisk the eggs then pour it into the frying pan while constantly stirring the eggs.

Add the chives when the eggs are almost cooked, allow it to cook for another minute or until the eggs are finally cooked.

Add in salt and pepper for flavor, then turn off heat and add in mushrooms, and pine nuts before serving.

Salmon and Zucchini Fritters

Ingredients

1 ½ cups of almond meal
2 eggs
100g of thinly sliced smoked salmon
1 tbsp chopped dill
2 roughly grated large zucchini with the liquid removed
Salt and pepper
1 tablespoon of oil

Instructions:

Combine the eggs and almond meal in a medium bowl, whisking both together until it is smooth.

Stir in the smoked salmon, dill, salt and pepper, and zucchini.

Place the oil in the frying pan over medium heat.

Spoon in approximately 1 tablespoonful of the smoked salmon combination into the frying pan. Make sure to allow it enough room for it to spread.

Fry the mixture for about 2-3 minutes on each side until completely cooked with a golden brown look.

Drain the fritter on either some absorbent paper or a paper towel.

Repeat the same process and add oil to the pan between each batch in order for it to cook properly.

Serve with a delicious green salad such as an arugula green salad.

Lemon Pancakes

2 eggs
1 tbsp of apple sauce
2 tbsp of lemon juice
1/3 cups of almond butter
1 tbsp of coconut oil

Instructions:

Combine all of the ingredients except for the coconut oil into a bowl.

Heat the coconut oil in medium heat in a frying pan.
Spoon the pancake mixture into the frying pan.

Fry the pancake for about 1 minute before flipping it over to the other side. Cook for 1 minute on the other side. Serve pancakes and enjoy.

Lunch Recipes

Dory Fillet with Beetroot Salad

Ingredients for the fish:

2 dory fillets
Lemon juice
Salt and pepper

Ingredients for salad:

½ small beetroot – diced finely
½ medium tomato – diced finely
1 cup finely chopped lettuce
5 chopped walnuts
Lemon juice

Instructions:

Preheat oven to 350°F degrees Fahrenheit.

Place the dory fillets in an oven tray and sprinkle it with salt, pepper and lemon juice.

Bake the fish in over for approximately 10-15 minutes.

For the salad, place all of the salad ingredients into a bowl combining them well and add in the lemon juice to taste. Serve the salad with fish and enjoy.

Cucumber Hot Dogs

Ingredients:

4 small sausages
4 small cucumbers
Tomato sauce (optional)

Instructions:

Preheat the grill medium/high heat.
Grill the sausages for about 6-8 minutes or until they are cooked thoroughly.

For the cucumber, cut the ends off the cucumbers and use a small knife or butter knife to remove the seeds by twisting the knife around in circles.

Place a hot sausage in the hollow part of the cucumber and serve with tomato sauce.

Dinner Recipes

Chicken Curry with Pumpkin

Ingredients

5 cups of diced pumpkin
Sliced 2 chicken breasts
2 tablespoons of olive oil
1 diced onion
2 finely chopped up garlic cloves
2 tablespoons of ground ginger
1 tablespoons of ground turmeric
2 tablespoons of ground coriander
2 tablespoons of ground cumin
Vegetable stock 1 ½ cups
1 small fresh heap of coriander, chopped
Add in a dash of salt.

Instructions

Put the diced onion and garlic into a pan, fry with the oil for at least 2-3 minutes on medium heat setting. Add in the sliced chicken and cook consistently stirring for about 10-11 minutes or until chicken has cooked thoroughly becoming white.

Add in the diced pumpkin, turmeric, ginger, cumin, and coriander. Stirring for at least 1 minute.

Add in the vegetable stock and allow it to simmer for approximately 15 minutes on low heat. Add in the chopped coriander, cover the pan and cook for about 2 minutes.

Add a dash of salt to taste.

Sides

Soups and Salads

Broccoli and Pine Nut Soup

Ingredients

1 diced onion
1 tablespoon of oil
3 cups of broccoli
3 cups of vegetable stock or chicken stock
¼ cup of pine nuts

Instructions:

Put the oil and diced onions in a large pan on medium heat until the onions are lightly browned.

Add in the stock and broccoli to the pan and let it simmer for approximately 10-15 minutes or until the broccoli has softened. Let the broccoli cool slightly.

Place the broccoli and stock into a food processor or use an electric blender if you don't own a food processor to create a smoother texture.

Heat the soup and serve.

Roast Vegetables in Orange and Rosemary

(Serves 4-6)

2 cups of diced pumpkin
2 tbsp of olive oil
2 cups of diced sweet potato
1 cup of diced carrots
1 juiced orange
6 tbsp of fresh rosemary leaves
2 finely chopped garlic cloves
Salt and pepper

Instructions

Pre-heat a fan-forced oven to 400 degrees Fahrenheit.

Combine all of the ingredients together and place into an oven proof dish
Bake in oven for 15 minutes. Remove from the oven and stir well to cover the vegetables in the orange liquid then return back to the oven for another 10-15 minutes or until the vegetables are tender.

Meats

Crunchy Sweet Potato Chips with Meatballs

Ingredients

Mince meat - 250g
Almond meal - 1/3 cup
Baby spinach – 3 cups
Tomato paste – approximately 25g
2 tablespoons of fresh sage
1 medium sweet potato
Olive oil
Salt to taste

Instructions

Preheat the oven to 350 degrees Fahrenheit.

Placing the spinach in a bowl, cover it with boiling water.
Cook spinach for 2 minutes before draining out as much liquid as possible from the spinach. Chop the spinach.

Place the mince meat, chopped spinach, almond meal, dash of salt, sage, and tomato paste. Combine the entire ingredients well.

Heat the frying pan to handle deep frying and peel the sweet potato with a vegetable peeler into ribbons.
Place a handful of the sweet potato ribbons into the frying pan for about 2 minutes. Allow them to brown slightly. Remove the cooked sweet potato ribbons and place on a plate with a paper towel on it to drain remaining oil.

Roll the mixture into 2.5cm size balls and place them on a baking tray lined with baking paper.

Bake in the oven for 10-15 minutes or until browned and cooked thoroughly.

On a plate place the meatballs with the sweet potato ribbons top of them.

Peppered Steak

Ingredients

4 - 100g rump steaks
Crushed peppercorns 4 tablespoons
1 beaten egg
1 tbsp oil

Instructions

Immerse the steak into the egg mixture, and then cover with crushed peppercorns.

Put the steak into pan or barbeque grill with some oil to grease. Fry on high setting for about 30 seconds on each side, then reduce down the heat and cook until steak is cooked tenderly.

Eat with boiled vegetables and/or crispy green salad.

Paprika Lamb

Ingredients

2- 400g cans diced tomatoes or 3 cups fresh tomatoes
2 tablespoons of olive oil
500g of lamb, diced
1 large onion, sliced thinly.
3 finely chopped garlic cloves
½ teaspoon caraway seeds
¼ cup of ground paprika

Instructions

With the oil in the pan add in the veal, set to medium heat and fry until browned. Save the pan juices to use as a sauce.

Remove veal from pan and add remaining oil along with garlic and onion. Put it on medium heating and cook veal for at least 4-5 minutes or until onions are soft. Add in the caraway seeds and paprika and stir for about 30 seconds.

Add in the veal and diced tomatoes to the pan, cover and leave to simmer for about an hour or until meat is tender and the sauce has thickened. If the sauce begins to dry then add in a little water to the mixture.

Moroccan Lamb with Squash

Ingredients

500g of lamb diced
1 tablespoon oil
Chicken or vegetable stock – 3 cups
1 tbsp ground cinnamon
3 cups of pumpkin diced
1 sliced onion
Cut into halves 6 yellow button squash
1 juiced lemon
1 tablespoon of honey
2/3 cups of prunes, pitted
Salt and pepper to taste

Instructions

In a pan heat oil, fry up the diced lamb until it has been cooked thoroughly.
Add in the chicken or vegetable stock and cinnamon. Cover the pan and simmer for at least an hour.

Add in the squash, onion, pumpkin, honey and lemon juice, then cover again and simmer for at least a half hour, or until vegetables have been cooked. Add in salt, pepper, and prunes, and cook for about 5 minutes. Allow it to cook before serving.

Poultry

Chicken with Macadamia Topping

Ingredients

2 teaspoons of olive oil
2 chicken breasts cut into 3 parts

For the Macadamia Topping:

1/3 cup of red onion diced
1 chopped finely garlic clove
1 teaspoon of the oil of your choice
Salt
½ cup of macadamia nuts
4 tablespoons of chives, chopped

Instructions

Put the pan on high setting, fry chicken with the oil. Cook the chicken for about 5-11 minutes or until the chicken is cooked thoroughly and browned. Cook both sides of the chicken.

For the macadamia topping, fry the onion, salt, garlic and oil separately until the nuts are soft and browned. Remove ingredients from the pan but leave the oil in it. Put the pan back on the heat and add in the macadamia nuts. Stir the nuts regularly until they are browned lightly. Use a blender to mix garlic and onion and nuts and pulse the blender until a crunchy texture has developed. Put the mixture into a bowl and combine in the chopped chives.

Sprinkle a sizeable amount of the macadamia combination over the chicken on a plate.

Serve the dish with steamed vegetables and a green salad.

Orange Chicken with Basil

2 tablespoons of olive oil
1 cup of orange juice, freshly squeezed (used oranges)
2 chicken breasts
Sea salt
Fresh basil 2/3 cup chopped roughly

Instructions

Pre-heat oven to 350º degrees Fahrenheit.

Using 2 pieces of baking paper place the chicken breasts into them. Bash the chicken breasts with a meat hammer until they are at least 1cm thick. Use a meat hammer or the end of a rolling pin and bash chicken breasts until 1cm thick.

Place the chicken breasts into an oven dish along and add in the basil, olive oil, orange juice, and a good dash of sea salt. Using aluminum foil, cover the oven dish tightly. Bake in oven for about 30-40 minutes, or until it is cooked thoroughly.

Serve with a salad or steamed vegetables.

Avocado Sauce with Baked Chicken

Ingredients:

Largely chopped pumpkin at least 3 cups
1 tablespoon of olive oil
2 chicken breast fillets
½ of an avocado
1 tablespoon of finely chopped fresh basil
Salt and pepper
1 cup of fresh rocket leaves
1 tablespoon of lemon juice

Instructions:

Pre-heat oven to 350º degrees Fahrenheit.

In an dish oven proof, put the pumpkin, salt and pepper, and olive oil. Bake for approximately 35-60 minutes or until completely cooked.

In medium heat, put the olive oil in a pan, fry chicken for about 4-8 minutes on each side or until cooked completely. Set the chicken aside for 5 minutes, then cutting across the grain, slice the chicken thinly.

In a blender or food processor, put the basil, lemon juice and avocado, pulse until a smooth paste has formed.

Put the chicken over the pumpkin and add the rocket leaves and add the avocado sauce.

Bombay Chicken Skewers

Ingredients

6 wooden skewers (soaked in cold water for about 20-30 minutes)
2 diced chicken breasts
4 tablespoons oil
2 tablespoons sweet paprika
1 tablespoon ground cumin
1 tablespoon ground coriander
2 finely chopped cloves of garlic
1 tablespoon ground turmeric

Instructions

Pre-heat oven to 350°degrees Fahrenheit or pre-heat grill on high setting.
To make sauce heat oil and spices in a frying pan on medium heat for 2-3 minutes, or until fragrant.

Line an oven tray with baking paper and then thread chicken on skewers. Coat chicken well with sauce.

Bake in oven for approximately 30-40 minutes, or until chicken has completely cooked.

Cook chicken for 4-7 minutes on each side if using a grill.

Rosemary and Lemon Chicken Skewers

Ingredients:

6 wooden skewers (soaked in cold water for about 20-30 minutes)
2 diced chicken breasts
2 tablespoons rosemary, finely chopped
2 tablespoons olive oil
1 tsp grated lemon rind
1/3 cup of lemon juice
Salt for taste

Instructions

Pre-heat oven to 350°degrees Fahrenheit or pre-heat BBQ grill on high.
Place rosemary, lemon rind, olive oil, lemon juice and salt in a small bowl and combine together.

Thread chicken on skewers and put in a tray oven proof lined with baking paper, coat the chicken with lemon sauce and rosemary. Bake in the oven for about 30-40 minutes, or until chicken has thoroughly cooked.

Cook chicken for 4-6 minutes on each side if cooking on a grill.

Snacks

Pistachio Salsa

Ingredients:

1/3 cup of toasted pistachios
1 cup finely diced tomatoes
1 finely chopped large garlic clove
1/3 cup of roughly chopped fresh parsley
2 finely chopped mint leaves,
1 tbsp of lemon juice
Dash of round paprika

Instructions:

Combine all ingredients in a bowl and mix together well.

Tomato Salsa

Ingredients:

1 cup finely diced tomato
¼ cup of finely chopped red onion
1 ½ tbsp of ground paprika
½ tsp of Mexican chili powder
1 tsp of finely chopped tarragon or oregano
1 tbsp lemon juice
1 tsp vinegar (optional)

Instructions:

Combine all ingredients in a bowl and mix together well.

Cashew Nut Dip

Ingredients:

2/3 cup of unsalted cashews
1 tbsp of olive oil
3 tbsp lemon juice
Salt and pepper for flavor

Instructions:

Use a blender to combine all of the ingredients together until a smooth paste has formed.

For a crunchy texture then blend the ingredients for a shorter period of time.

Desserts

Blueberry Sorbet
Ingredients
2 cups blueberries
½ medium banana
1/3 cup of coconut milk
1½ tbsp honey
1 egg white, beaten until stiff peaks have formed

Instructions

Use a blender to blend together blueberries, banana, coconut milk and honey until well combined.

Fold blueberry mixture into the beaten egg white. Pour into an ice-cream container or a freezer proof container and freeze for approximately 6 hours or overnight until set.

To serve, cut into slices.

Stir in shredded coconut and then fold mixture into the beaten egg white.

Pour the mixture into an ice-cream container / freezer proof container and freeze for approximately 6 hours or overnight until set.

To serve, cut into slices and enjoy.

Mixed Berry Compote

Ingredients

2 tea bags herbal tea, such as chamomile, orange tea, jasmine
1 freshly squeezed orange
2 cups mixed berries

Instructions

Place tea bags and orange juice in a saucepan and simmer over low heat for 1 minute.

Add in the berries and allow it to simmer until berries are juicy and plump.

Take out the tea bags.

Cover and refrigerate for several hours prior to serving.

Paleolithic Cookbook Conclusion

The Paleolithic diet isn't a diet that is going to fade away but instead will continue to grow as more people gain knowledge about the full benefits of the diet. The fundamentals of the paleolithic diet provide dieters with the needed guidelines and principles to apply to our daily life and lifestyle. Our ancestors' diet may have varied as it depended on where they lived along with their environmental climates and other factors involved. Ancestors living around Canada would more likely eat fresh salmon, deer, berries and plants. Ancestors living in Africa would eat animals and plant roots. Aboriginals in Australia would live off the land eating plants, bugs, native nuts, honey and animals. Remember our ancestors ate well and were in good health and this same diet will provide the exact same benefits for us.

Baby Food Diet
Achieve Weight Loss With The Baby Food Diet

Part I: Getting Started with Weight Loss

Myself I've had difficulty with weight loss all my life. I've never been able to lose those pounds no matter how hard I tried. I worked on different diets and different exercise plans and still had no success. I felt all the frustration that you're feeling right now. I've searched over and over for the right diet for me. I've even tried practically every crazy diet plan out there. I finally found this diet and realized that it actually worked.

This diet uses something extremely simple to help you get fit fast. In fact, it uses something you've probably never thought about eating as an adult, baby food. When I started following this diet and exercising regularly I started shedding pounds fast. This is a very naturalistic diet for most people and it helps you to eat healthier, foods with more nutrients.

Buying baby food from the store is the easy way to go about this diet however there are plenty of other ways to follow it as well. You'll be able to create your own diet plan and keep yourself healthier than ever. You'll also be eating something completely homemade which means you'll be eating foods with more nutritional value and less preservatives and additives. I myself enjoy making my own baby food because it allows me to exercise complete control over what I eat.

Remember that losing weight may be your ultimate goal but at the same time you want to make sure that you're giving your body a healthy diet that promotes good things in your entire body. When you make your own food you're actually achieving this goal much faster and you're helping your body in more ways than you could even imagine.

Chapter 1- Watch for Weight Loss Dangers

No matter where you look there are weight loss plans and programs staring back at you. You've probably seen them on TV every time you turn it on and you see them online when you visit your favourite sites. They're in movies and magazines. Everywhere you look there are weight loss programs of different types and those ads make it confusing for you to get started. You probably don't know which diets are actually good for you or which will work. Well, that's why it's important to understand what we're about to discuss right here.

You see there are a wide variety of weight loss programs that will work. That's right you did read that correctly. Many of those weight loss programs will work. The problem is that you have to follow them exactly which is likely either a) extremely difficult or b) extremely dangerous. That's why you should really carefully consider every weight loss program before you decide to try it and you should check out these common practices in weight loss programs.

Danger 1) Fasting

One of the most common and most dangerous methods of losing weight is through fasting. Many people have done this and many so-called health programs and diets tout this option for fast weight loss. For this to work the individual must starve themselves daily so that they are capable of losing weight. If this sounds like the definition of eating disorders then you're reading it right. This is generally what happens with people who have eating disorders. You want to make sure that it doesn't happen to you.

Remember that fasting or starving tends to lead to disastrous consequences. Someone who starves their body is actually causing it to waste away. This means that you'll lose the weight but your body will start to shut down at the same time. You're going to become extremely unhealthy because your body is going to try and save itself when it thinks that it's dying. Your body turns on your weight loss goals when that happens.

In order to get healthy and lose weight at the same time you need to make sure that you are following a healthy and balanced lifestyle and diet. People can die from these types of fasting or extreme exercise diets. It's actually happened before and you don't want to be just another statistic now do you? Of course not. You want to actually succeed at your goal and then go on to have new goals.

If you starve yourself your body starts to struggle to survive. It's not getting the nutrients that it needs so it starts taking from the parts of your body that it considers to be unnecessary. So your protein and water start to disappear. Your muscle mass is where that protein is stored so anywhere you currently have muscle is going to go away. The soft feeling of your skin is going to go away as well since your body needs that water and can't afford to expend it making you look nice.

Now we get to the part you want to get rid of, your fat. Well when you don't eat your body doesn't get any more fat and that means that the fat it does have is important. That fat keeps you alive and so the body stores it instead of burning it off. You'll have a higher chance of type 2 diabetes and other health problems as well because your body will be increasing fat and decreasing everything else. You'll have a difficult time getting your mind and body to work the way you want them to because you simply don't have the energy.

Danger 2) Weight Loss Pills

Over the counter pills, drops and supplements promise pretty much everything these days. They promise that you'll lose weight, reverse baldness, get ripped and basically anything and everything else. That means you should be even more careful than normal. You want to make sure you're getting healthy the right way. Health supplements are sold in stores and online. They're also made of pretty much anything and everything available on the market which means not only do many of them not work but a large number of them can actually be dangerous.

Look at who is making those supplements. Do you even know the company? Many pills aren't even created with a brand. Many of the pills may not even have a real name, just a chemical name or compound. A lot of those pills are also not approved by the FDA (Food and Drug Administration) which means that they don't have to adhere to any type of safety guidelines or any type of honesty claims. They could be complete lies or made of ingredients that are harmful.

Before you go thinking that you should be safe because you're purchasing the products legally think about this, products that are sold don't have to be evaluated by the FDA. That means you can purchase the product legally from pretty much anywhere but that doesn't mean that it's safe for you to take. 'Cures' are the only things that actually *have* to be reviewed so as long as it doesn't claim to cure your problem it could be made of anything and made by anybody. That means stay away from anything that isn't specifically provided or prescribed by your doctor.

Of course this brings us to herbal supplements. Herbs are good for you right? They have to be safe and they'll only be helpful even if they don't actually help you in your weight loss goals. Actually those are all false. Herbs can be good for you and they can provide help with different health problems. They are not miracle workers however and, just like anything else, they can actually be dangerous in certain conditions.

Vitamins and minerals are healthy for you. Vitamin A, Vitamin B, Iron, Magnesium … all of these things can be taken (after talking with your doctor and ensuring you're getting the right amounts) without concern. Herbal supplements that promise weight loss or health cures however are very different. These supplements are actually made of diuretics and caffeine. That means they aren't going to do much but keep you going and make you go to the bathroom more often.

Caffeine helps to keep you moving. You may notice people who drink a lot of soda or coffee or even energy drinks to stay away, maybe you're one of those people. Well those things are full of caffeine which gives you a bit of an energy boost. Diuretics make you go to the bathroom more frequently than normal. This can actually be extremely unhealthy because it changes the levels of electrolytes in your body. A change in electrolytes can actually send you to the hospital. Another thing is that diuretics cause dehydration because you're going to the bathroom so frequently and it's easy to become dehydrated without even realizing it.

Talk with your doctor about these supplements. What you'll likely hear is that they are quick fixes that will help you to lose weight quickly but in a dangerous way that won't even last long term. Losing weight the healthy way can cause you to live longer and healthier. It means that your body actually works like it's younger than it is because it gets more nutrients and feels better than before. But you need to eat right and you need to exercise. You don't need to be taking some herbal supplement that causes your body harm.

If you've found a suspicious or dangerous supplement then you should get ahold of the FDA right away. This can be done at
http://www.fda.gov/Safety/ReportaProblem/ucm059315.htm.

This will ensure that others don't get hurt by those dangerous pills or supplements. Programs and diets that encourage you to take pills or supplements like the HCG diet are also not healthy for you. They can cause many different problems and true dieticians will tell you to avoid them.

Danger 3) Detox

Have you heard all the different health programs that advocate detoxing? Well this may seem like a great idea but it's not, at least not if you're doing it at home without medical supervision. Detox when done properly can be good for you. It can help you to get healthier and help prepare your body for future weight loss as well. The problem is that it can cause dehydration which can be dangerous when not carried out in a health care facility under supervision.

These processes do nothing to help you stop gaining weight however since they actually have nothing to do with the reasons that you're gaining. They won't help you with your eating habits and they definitely won't keep your healthy. You could actually end up dehydrated and with an irregular heartbeat as well. So you're not going to get the health benefits you think you will.

As far as getting rid of toxins goes your body already knows how to do that. You may not know it but your body is extremely smart. It knows how to get rid of the waste that you put into it and it knows how to expel the waste it needs to survive. It doesn't need you to help with that process which means you don't need to start a cleansing program.

If you want to help your body with this process anyway there is a simple way to do it that's also healthy. Eat more fiber. Eating fiber helps your body to detox the right way. You won't have to worry about dehydrating yourself (at least not as much though you'll still want to drink plenty of water). You also won't have to worry about nasty side effects because you'll be eating foods like avocado and grain which are the perfect ways to eat healthy, get detox benefits and help your body.

Danger 4) Purging

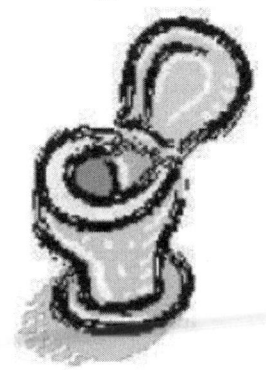

Purging is the expelling of something forcefully. It is extremely dangerous for a great number of reasons and should never be done. Ever. This tends to go right alongside starvation in the danger front and generally those who engage in one will engage in the other. Many people tend to follow this 'weight loss program' because it's far easier than watching what you eat. We won't deny that it's easy to purge and it does have fast results. What we're going to tell you however are all about the negative results that come fast as well.

When you purge your food you are also purging the stomach acid that is trying to break down that food. That acid comes through your throat and it is highly corrosive. That means it corrodes your esophagus. It also corrodes your teeth. Purging can actually increase your chances of cancer because of all of these negative affects. The more you do it the worse off your body will be and that's definitely not something you want.

If you ever feel compulsions to purge or feel like you have to purge you need to get help. This is a sign of an eating disorder and it is imperative that you get help from a medical professional immediately.

Danger 5) Over-Exercise

Exercise is good for you but if you find yourself doing it more and more then you probably have a problem. Doing anything too much can cause harm and that extends to anything you think is good for you as well. Too much of one vitamin is bad for you. Too much ice cream is bad for you and too much exercise is definitely bad for you. You should not be exercising more than two hours a day and no more than three hours at the absolute most if you are a sports enthusiast.

According to the American Heart Association and the American Academy of Sports Medicine the optimum amount of time to exercise is 30 minutes a day, seven days a week. Of course you should be doing either 20 minutes of cardio each day or 30 minutes five out of seven days. Too much of this can cause problems for your body but too little won't get you the results that you want. High intensity training about three times a week can help you to burn more calories and increase your heart rate without wearing you out too fast.

Two days a week you should be working on strength exercises with 8-12 repetitions and 10+ different exercises. This helps you get the most out of your exercise time even though it may seem like you're not working out very much. These exercises will help to improve your strength and your shape. They'll also help you feel stronger and feel ready for whatever comes your way.

Danger 6) Drugs

Whether they're the legal kind or not, drugs can be very bad for you when you use them to lose weight. Many people like to misuse their prescriptions or someone else's prescriptions simply because one of the side effects is weight loss. This can be extremely dangerous. You should never take a prescription medication that is not specifically prescribed to you and you should never take that prescription for anything other than its intended use. Abusing medications can cause nearly every health problem you could imagine including strokes or kidney problems.

Danger 7) Tobacco

You may have heard that smoking can supress your appetite. Well this is actually true. The problem is that it's not healthy in any way. Smoking causes lung problems, heart disease, cancer and practically every other health problem under the sun. There are no health benefits associated with smoking. Not even one. So make sure you don't start this awful habit and that you work towards quitting if you're already addicted. The longer you wait the harder it gets.

Chapter 2- Start Watching Calories

Lowering your caloric intake is one way that you can start losing weight. It's also one of the safest ways that you can lose weight. What you need to do is look online for ways that you can still eat the types of foods that you love without getting quite as many calories. You'd be amazed how many different recipes there are that will taste great and give you a lower caloric intake. What you should know however, is that you don't have to buy those low calorie foods online, you can make them.

There is no such thing as a miracle drug or ingredient when it comes to losing weight or watching your calories. So don't get tricked into buying something that's only going to slow you down in the long run. You're going to need to put some time and effort into your weight loss or it simply isn't going to work. Here's what you need to know if you're planning to start watching your calories.

Talk to Your Doctor

Your doctor knows more about you than you do. They know and understand your body and how it works. They also know about your health conditions, your medications and more. They also know if you need to lose weight and how best you should go about it. So make sure you clue them in about what you should be doing. They'll be able to tell you more information than you'd be able to get for yourself.

Your doctor is the one that will give you your BMI which tells you whether you are currently a healthy weight, overweight or underweight. This can help you to make plans to start dieting. Remember that your body weight accounts for your fat content and muscle content so don't think just because your number is high it means something bad. If you're a bodybuilder for example your BMI is going to be higher because all that muscle weighs a lot. The true test is going to be your percent of body fat.

Chapter 3- Necessary Calories

Your body needs calories in order to function but it only needs so many. The rest are calories that truly just turn into fat and cause you to gain more weight. So that means if you want to lose weight or get to a healthier weight then you need to understand what that magic number is. How many calories does your body absolutely need (you don't want to go below this number) and how many is too many?

If you're trying to lose weight you need to reduce the number of calories that you take in. Ideally you'll decrease your intake by 100 to 500 calories and not any more than this. You'll want to talk with your doctor to find out more and you'll want to keep your intake above 1,200 unless your doctor tells you otherwise. If you do this on your own it could cause you disastrous health problems because too few calories causes your body to rebel.

Taking in too few calories can cause dizziness, irritability, lack of focus and hunger. That's because your body doesn't know how to function on less than a set number of calories and if you aren't getting that number then your body starts cutting off the unnecessary functions to preserve the necessary ones, like breathing and keeping your heart beating. So keep enough calories in your body at all times.

It may seem complicated to count your calories and definitely to reduce them since that means eating less than you're used to. The easiest thing to do is just start small. Cut out a snack or two each day or each slightly less at each meal. As your body adjusts you'll feel better throughout the day and you won't even notice the lesser amounts of food.

Remember that reducing your calories and going out losing weight the healthy way takes time. You're going to need to exercise hard and start cutting calories and you're going to have to wait to see the results. It's going to take time and you may not even notice the change because it will be so gradual.

Another important thing to keep in mind is that it's difficult to lose weight. So don't set a goal to lose 100 pounds and then expect to achieve it fast. What you want to do is set small goals that are attainable. Start with something that's extremely easy and you know you can do, like cutting out one snack each day. That's easy right? You can do it just by remembering it. So then when you manage to cut out that one snack every day for an entire week you can consider that goal reached. Then gradually start making your goals more difficult to achieve so you have to work a little harder at them.

When you work your way up to it you can reduce 200 calories from your diet and you will barely even notice it. But your body will definitely start showing the results and that will help you feel better and stick to your new diet that much better as well. Which means your results will show up faster. So you see it's a great cycle that just keeps working to help you look and feel your best.

Chapter 4- Proper Way to Count Calories

Counting calories isn't the easiest thing to do. In fact it requires a lot of knowledge, a lot of research and you measuring out the amount of food that you eat. You're going to need to use measuring cups and keep the amount of food you're eating to exact serving sizes which means you need to pay attention to food labels.

Keeping track of the amount of calories in the foods you eat can be simple if you're eating something like a cup of cereal because there's a food label on the side of the package that says you're getting a certain amount of calories per serving. What can be difficult is eating prepared meals or home cooked meals. These often have different calorie amounts than the individual foods that make them up which is where your smartphone or internet come into play. You want to make sure you're counting right so you don't take in too many calories without realizing it.

Remember that anything you drink has calories in it as well. This means that the salad you ordered for lunch may be great and it may fall below your calorie limit but the two sodas you drink with it will push you over your limit. Remember all those calories in your drinks the next time you sit down to have a meal.

The best thing to do is drink a lot of tea (natural not sweetened), water or fresh juices. You can actually invest in a juicing machine for yourself and start making your own juices which are great for your entire body. We're not going to discuss too much about this process here but you should know that it will help your body get more of the nutrients that it needs without all the additives.

Chapter 5- Record What You Eat

If you write down your food and drink intake each day it will help you keep track of your calories much easier. You'll be able to better understand what you're eating and what it can do for or against you. It may seem complicated or annoying at first but it definitely can have its benefits and even though it's time consuming it will get you into shape better and faster than you might think possible.

You have many choices when it comes to keeping a food journal. You could choose to get a notebook or journal that you can write in with a pen and carry around with you everywhere. You may want to keep notes on your smartphone or laptop or you may even want to get an app that records all of these things. There are even some software programs or online resources (both paid and unpaid) that will help you keep track of what you eat and drink each day. Many of these sources will also break down the different food groups you are eating from and display patterns in your eating habits.

A food journal can be very helpful if you're not seeing the type of results you had hoped for or expected. In this case you can look back at your food log and see what you've been doing so you can find problems or discrepancies in your log. Remember you need to record absolutely everything that you eat and drink and not just the things you want to remember. So if you splurge on a candy bar in the middle of the day you still need to write that down.

If you are following your diet (which your journal will show) and you're still not losing weight you'll be able to go talk to your doctor and find out if there is a medical problem that is keeping you from losing. Make sure you're also exercising the right amount to get rid of the excess calories and fat that your body does take in as well or you'll have a hard time staying in shape even if the fat does start coming off.

Chapter 6- What You Should Eat

Taking in the right types of food is what's going to help you lose the weight. That's because your diet accounts for about 80% of your weight loss and your exercise accounts for about 20%. So eating right is more important than exercising enough (though you'll still need that exercise). Even your personal trainer would attest to the importance of eating healthy.

If you eat the wrong types of foods you can actually continue to gain weight even though you're eating less food simply because you're eating the wrong types of food. You need to watch your portion sizes, count your calories, limit your carbs and more all at the same time. Neglecting just one of these can cause you to miss your calorie goals and gain weight.

When you decrease the amount of calories that you eat it means you need to increase the amount of nutrition for each of those calories. You're going to need to get vitamins and minerals in all of the foods that you eat or you could end up having more problems than you're solving from your diet. Those vitamins and minerals help you to improve your body all the way from the top of your head to your toes so don't neglect them. You need to eat every color of the rainbow and every letter of the alphabet (not to mention minerals too).

Don't forget that junk food and fast food are full of empty calories which means you get a lot of calories and very few (if any) benefits from vitamins or minerals. These are the foods to avoid. More foods to avoid are fatty meats and processed food. Whole foods and fruits and vegetables are your best bet and these should be eaten even more because you'll get more vitamins and minerals for each calorie that you're taking in.

If you're eating something that is processed then you're getting salt, fat and sugar usually in high quantities. These are important to have in your body but you don't need a lot of them. In fact, you need very little of them. Too much salt keeps your body from getting rid of water which causes you to gain weight. Too much fat is just that, more fat and too much sugar will turn into more fat. So think about why you should be avoiding these foods and then do it.

It may seem impossible for you to cook meals every single day that are going to be healthy. After all between work and school and kids and family and spouses and friends you don't have a lot of time right? Well there are recipes online that will help you to prepare healthy meals for you and your family in only a short amount of time. You'll save money and you'll help your body and your weight loss goals all at the same time.

All you'll need is 20 to 30 minutes of your time and your meals will be all made up. If you have a crock pot this can be even easier because all you need to do is cut up your ingredients and you'll be able to go about your normal routine without having to worry about the food until it's time to eat. It's fast, it's easy and you can eat whenever you want. Of course that are some important things to keep in mind when you're trying to stay healthy.

1. Get rid of things that don't fit. If it doesn't fit into your diet then get rid of it. Having it around the house will cause you to break the rules simply because it's there. Don't tempt yourself. Ditch everything that could tempt you to break your diet. It could be anything from snacks to sweets or even processed meats. Keep them from sneaking into your grocery cart next time you go shopping as well.

2. Buy plenty of fruits and veggies. These are healthy for you and they'll keep your diet tasting good as well. There are so many different types of fruits and veggies that you won't get bored with them and you'll always be able to find some that you like. Make sure you like everything in your fridge however, if you don't like it then you won't eat it no matter how healthy it is. Also stock some lean proteins.

3. Eat more seafood. Beef and pork are full of fats and are good things to cut out of your diet. So instead try adding some seafood in. You'll get a lot more omega 3 fatty acids this way (which is good for your diet) and you'll get a lot less fats.

4. Check your weight every other week. When you check your weight you'll be able to see how you're doing on your weight loss goals. You'll also be able to start making slight changes to your weight loss plans and goals because you'll slowly be achieving that goal. Remember however that when you change your calorie intake to accommodate a change in weight you'll also need to change your exercise for the same reason. Don't be afraid to go back to your doctor and see what they have to say about anything.

5. Stress can be your worst enemy. Make sure that you aren't getting too stressed out with your diet and juggling everything you need to do. It's easy to find a moment of time in the day that you can prepare your meals so they are ready when you're ready to eat. A lot of people don't actually have time to prepare something when they're ready to eat and so they eat something unhealthy that's just quick. So make up your meals while you do have the time so they're ready when you don't. Make foods that can easily be stored in the refrigerator and heated when you're ready.

6. Shop where you normally do. You don't need to go to an organic food store to get healthy foods. Your normal supermarket carries fruits and veggies too and that means you can keep your normal shopping plan. You don't need to change everything to get healthy. If you want to try out the organic shop down the road go right ahead but remember organic food prices are often more expensive. A change to your normal routine is also just that, a change and it's not likely to stay. You're probably going to go back to your supermarket in a few days or even a week and that means you'll stop buying the healthy foods because you didn't create a habit at your normal shop.

7. Drink water. The average person is actually supposed to drink six or more glasses of water every single day. You should also be eating foods that have water in them. This helps you to lose the weight you want to lose and also ensures that you stay healthy while you do so. You won't have to change too much (switch out at least one other beverage for water) and you'll get better results much faster.

Part II: The Baby Food Diet

So now you've learned what you need to know about dieting in general. You understand the different steps involved and you know how to keep the process going. You understand how to stay healthy while you lose weight and how to stick to your plans and your goals. Well in this section we're going to talk specifically about the baby food diet so you can better understand what it is and what you need to do in order to follow it and lose weight.

Knowing the basics first is instrumental to following a diet because you need to know the ins and outs of dieting before you jump in feet first. Otherwise how would you know what to expect? Your body is a well-tuned machine and it's crucial that you do everything you can to help it run properly. That's why the first section of this book was focused on dieting in general and how to get you healthy.

The baby food diet is just starting to get popular which means that it's not advertised in magazines or books at this point (other than this one anyway). It is, however, slowly becoming one of the more popular diets even up there with Weight Watchers and Atkins. So don't go thinking this is one of those fad diets we warned you about earlier in this book.

It's unclear who invented the baby food diet. It has, however, been used by celebrities including (rumor has it) Madonna and her trainer Tracy Anderson. Still who has used it and when doesn't matter as much as why you should use it or what it's going to do for you. What it will do is get you ready for beach season and help you to stay slim throughout the rest of the year as well.

This diet uses whole ingredients to keep you healthy. If you choose to purchase baby food from the supermarket you'll still be getting healthier products and ingredients than you likely would in your normal diet. Manufacturers are taking care to keep their products healthy because parents are starting to get more and more particular about what is being given to their infants. This bodes well for you however because it means the diet is healthier than ever. There are three main benefits to this diet which are as follows:

1. Increases the number of meals the dieter eats in a day.

2. Decreases the amount of calories taken in.

3. Easier to eat special foods on the go.

Chapter 7- How the Diet Works

If you want to go all in and get the fastest and best results from this diet then you'd replace all of your meals with baby food. You would eat one jar 14 times per day which may mean one per hour (babies eat quite frequently remember). This is considered pretty extreme however and is not the most popular method of following this diet.

If you only need to change up your diet a little you can replace your snacks with a jar of baby food. This is typically for those who are already eating relatively healthy and simply need to cut back on some junk food or heavy snacking throughout the day. You'll be able to lose some weight and get in better shape without too big of a change to your normal routine.

If you eat a lot of calories in a day then you'll want to start replacing your biggest meals with baby food instead. If you eat a heavy lunch every day then replace this meal with baby food and follow your normal diet for the rest of your day. This will help you to cut back without cutting out too much of the food that your body needs to get through the day.

The amount of calories you take in is important because it will affect your weight and what happens to it. If you eat more calories than normal you'll maintain your weight for a time and then gain weight. If you eat fewer calories than normal you'll begin to lose weight. That's the goal of this diet (and any other healthy diet) and that's what you need to focus on the most.

This diet doesn't force you to follow a lot of rules and in fact a lot of it is up to interpretation. You can eat your regular meals and substitute in baby food whenever you feel it's appropriate. Make sure you measure the amount of food and drink that you take in each day (and the amount of baby food). Don't take in more calories than you are supposed to and make sure that you are continuing to keep track of the calories that you need and have taken at all times.

You don't need to be able to 'eyeball it' when you're measuring out portions. You can invest in an inexpensive kitchen scale and some measuring cups to help you out and to keep you eating the right way. After some time you'll be a little better at spotting how much food you're eating and understanding portion sizes without having to measure out the ingredients.

Chapter 8- Why Baby Food?

You may be wondering why anyone would choose to follow this diet. It may seem strange and you're probably wondering where this diet came from. Well you'll find that there are few people actually endorsing the diet be they celebrities or scientists. You'll also find that there is very little that's actually special about this particular diet as well. All that you need to know is that counting calories will help you to lose weight.

The baby food diet will not speed up your metabolism and it won't help you burn fat or sugar. It won't even decrease your appetite. What it's going to do is ensure that you will eat fewer calories throughout the day and that you won't feel starved from missing meals or snacks that your body is used to. It's also helpful because your body will be almost continuously breaking down food which means that you won't feel hungry. All it takes is control over the amount of calories that you take in each day.

Fast food can really mess up your diet because you can't easily count the number of calories that are in those meals. As a result, you tend to eat more calories than you should which causes you to actually gain weight. This is why it's important to exercise properly, count calories, eat baby food when you feel compelled to eat larger meals and avoid as much junk food or fast food as you possibly can. These things will help you to cut down on your weight.

One jar of baby food is about 100 calories and if you stick with this diet full time you'll be eating around 1,000 to 1,400 calories each day. This means you get plenty of food without eating too many calories. Some types of this food even have fewer calories than that which means you can eat even more without getting too many.

Another option with baby food is to eat certified organic versions. These can be slightly more expensive but they have even more health benefits and likely even less calories. So remember that you'll get more good things than bad out of eating these foods and you'll definitely start feeling better faster than you might have imagined possible.

If you want to really get the best benefits possibly you can make your own baby food. This can be a little more complicated but it doesn't have to be too much. We've even included some recipes for you at the end of this book so you don't have to look them up yourself. But what's important to understand are the general contents that are included in baby food.

- Carbohydrates – 11.6 grams

- Fiber – 1.8 grams

- Sugar – 3.3 grams

- Fat – 0.7 grams

- Saturated fat - 0.1 grams

- Monounsaturated fat – 0.2 grams

- Polyunsaturated fat – 0.3 grams

- Omega 3 fatty acids – 38.5 milligrams

- Omega 6 fatty acids – 231 milligrams

- Protein – 1.9 grams

Baby food also contains the following trace nutrients:
- Vitamin A

- Vitamin C

- Vitamin D

- Vitamin E

- Vitamin K

- Thiamin

- Riboflavin

- Niacin

- Vitamin B6

- Folate

- Vitamin B12

- Pantothenic acid

- Choline

- Betaine

This means that you're going to get a lot of healthy nutrients that your body needs without getting too many calories. You'll get a nutrient dense meal that keeps you full. If you prefer there's ways to make some healthy meals at home which are also nutrient dense but this is much more complicated and tends to increase the problems associated with calorie counting.

There are some important things to understand about this diet and we're going to explain them right here.

1. Eat baby food that is commercially made or homemade. This is the only rule associated with this diet and it's a relatively easy one to follow because you only eat as much baby food as you feel you need when you feel that you need it.

2. Make sure that you're counting calories because this is going to prove crucial to your being able to get healthy and lose weight. You need to be in control of the calories that you take in and that means knowing the exact number at all times. Portion control is a part of calorie counting so if anyone tells you just to stick with certain portion sizes you're still counting calories just not quite in the same way.

3. You need a little room to grow in your diet. No one can stick to a super strict diet all the time and absolutely avoid all unhealthy foods or additives. Some people may claim they can but very few actually are able to. Don't worry if you splurge once in a while and have a cheeseburger or a soda. These little flaws are completely normal and you'll still be able to lose some weight. Find out from your doctor or a trainer what level of splurging or 'cheating' on diets is normal and you'll likely be surprised at the answer.

It can be difficult to follow a diet and that's generally why people cheat a little towards the beginning especially. Don't worry if you find yourself having difficulty sticking to your diet towards the beginning. Try your hardest to do so and keep working at it. Even if you gradually start the diet you'll be reaching your goals faster than if you decide you have to do everything cold turkey.

Keep yourself healthy and start your diet and exercise plan the right way. You definitely don't want to keep putting it off because it's definitely not doing you any good that way. You're just keeping yourself from reaching your goals and your dreams.

This diet is all about what you want and when you want it. If you want to follow it strictly you're more than welcome too but then if you're not interested in following quite as much you're welcome to do that as well. Eat what you want to and when you want to. Don't expect to do something you don't really want to do.

Chapter 9- Expert Opinions

Knowing what the experts think is very important. After all, they're experts for a reason. I look up absolutely everything I can find to determine if a diet is healthy or not and then I make sure that the experts agree with the diet. I know that you probably want more than just my opinion on whether or not this diet is going to be good for you and that's why I'm going to include some of the opposing points to this diet and why they don't really matter or why they can be refuted. After all, they most definitely can be refuted and you'll want to know how so you can support this diet yourself.

1. Baby food is created for babies and doesn't have the nutritional requirements to feed adults.

This is true because baby food is made for babies and it includes the nutrients that a growing baby would need. Unfortunately that doesn't include a lot of the nutrients that adults need like protein. The way to avoid this problem is to supplement your current diet with baby food. As long as you don't switch 100% over to eating just baby food you will get the nutrients that you need (that aren't provided by the food) from the rest of your diet. This way you'll be able to get the nutrients you need but not all the extras.

2. Eating baby food makes the body feel deprived.

This is true as well but for a reason you may not think. Your body can actually get tired of not chewing your feed. If you eat a lot of foods that typically require a lot of chewing then this diet could give you more problems on this. There are, however, ways to get around this and to accommodate your body.

Set low goals and only slowly switch to eating baby food rather than jumping all in. You can't really make a crazy extensive goal and expect to stick to it anyway. You won't be healthy that way. Whatever weight your body may be at this is what your body considers to be normal. So if you weigh 100 pounds your body won't want you to lose weight (which is good) but if you weigh 300 pounds your body also won't want you to lose weight.

It believes that this is normal and that you shouldn't be taking anything away. You'll encounter resistance to your goals. As you continue to work at it however your body will eventually let go of those pounds and allow you to create a new normal.

If the baby food isn't satisfying you then reward yourself. Not with all those unhealthy foods you normally eat but with vegetables, grain, fruits and lean protein. Have a big meal at the end of the day but keep it healthy. When you eat more fiber and nutrients you actually feel more full. This is because those ingredients keep you full but also because you can eat more of them without overloading your calorie count.

The next idea is to alternate your days of eating baby food. Only eat it a few days a week and then the other days just stick to a healthy diet of fruits and veggies without all the added sugar and caffeine.

3. How do you eat those weird flavors?

Okay baby food does come in some odd flavors and combinations. And sometimes it just doesn't seem very appetizing when you're hungry. But if you try out different types of baby food you'll be able to find the ones that you really like and you'll be able to cut your portions. That means the diet won't take too long and you'll be able to do it by just adding a few simple (albeit a little strange) ingredients to your daily food routine.

With this diet you have the freedom to decide what you do and don't eat. You have the ability to adjust what you're eating and how much. That's not very common with other diet plans and it's definitely something you should be very happy about with this one.

In order to make this diet work for you you're going to have to create a healthy relationship with food. If you use it to cope with your problems or to handle emotions you're not going to be able to follow this diet very easily. You're going to have some problems sticking to eating healthy. If you have a healthy relationship with your food however, you'll be able to lose weight easily.

Chapter 10- What You Should Know About the Baby Food Diet

Just like anything else there are advantages and disadvantages of the baby food diet. These are things that you should know before you get started because they may impact whether or not you decide to follow this diet for yourself. So here goes:

Advantages:

- Baby food includes large amounts of many of the nutrients you need including vitamins and minerals.

- Baby food can be bought absolutely anywhere.

- Baby food can be homemade specific to your tastes.

- It has low fat, salt and sugar.

- It helps to maintain your weight.

- This diet is more flexible than other diet plans.

- You can easily control your caloric intake because you're eating one jar which is already pre-measured.

- Baby food helps to regulate your cravings.

- This is a low calorie substitute for other snacks or junk food.

- You won't need to cook.

- There are no health risks involved with eating baby food.

Disadvantages:

- You may feel hungry and unsatisfied from the flavor, lack of texture and lack of chewing.

- This diet can be expensive if you are on a tight budget.

- This food could be considered strange to outsiders and they may not understand your new diet or how it works.

- You'll likely have an urge to overeat at your next meal because of the lack of texture in the baby food.

- You may have difficulty following this diet for extended periods of time.

Chapter 11- How to Succeed

It may seem difficult to succeed at your plans especially after reading through some of this. The truth is that eating healthy can seem difficult and even making a plan to eat healthy is very difficult for most people. So congratulations you've already made one step in the right direction. You've already decided that it's important to be healthy and to keep your body healthy. So that means you're already on the road to success. These tips will help you even more on your plans:

1. Be positive-negativity is your biggest enemy. It keeps you from succeeding at the things you want to do in life and it definitely stops you from reaching your weight loss goals. You need to support yourself and that means encouraging yourself that you really can do this. You need to believe that you can exercise each day and that you can eat properly. If you don't you simply can't. It's really that easy. Your attitude matters a lot.

2. Get rid of unhealthy habits-Here's the thing about habits; you do them without thinking about them. That's what makes them a habit. So that means it can take some time to go about changing those habits. You have to consciously think about what you're doing and consciously change to do something else. Make sure you are working towards that change because you're definitely going to need it. You may even need professional help if you're having difficulty with your habit changes. Make sure you make those

changes because you definitely can't afford to have those bad habits keeping you from reaching your goals.

3. Find a friend-Changing your diet and your habits can be very difficult. So find someone that wants to meet the same goals that you do. Get them to help you by helping them. Make goals together and then set about reaching those goals together. You'll definitely have an easier time of it because you're not alone. You'll also be more likely to reach your goals because you have someone there to help you and encourage you when you feel like you can't go on. You could find one or more friends who share your ideas and go for it.

4. Make a commitment-once you make that commitment it can make it easier for you to reach your goals though you may not think so. All you need to do is write down your goal on a piece of paper and that commitment will be ingrained in your head. Once you write your goals down it makes them more concrete to you and that can be very important to reaching your ultimate goal.

5. Like healthy food-once you decide that you actually like the taste of healthy food it can be much easier to stay healthy. That's because your taste buds decide more of what you like and don't like and they are a large part of why you gain weight, you eat what tastes good rather than what's good for you. If you decide that healthy food does taste good then you'll be better off. You don't need to completely give up the unhealthy foods but you should definitely cut back on how much of them you're eating. That means you should only allow your diet to consist of unhealthy food about 20% of the time. Everything else should be lean protein, fresh fruit and veggies.

6. Enjoy your exercise-if you like to exercise you'll do it more often and that bodes well for your health plans. Don't think about going to the gym as this terrible place where you're going to hate yourself and your time there. If you go to a gym you'll find it's not as bad as all that but you don't even have to do that. You can actually exercise in a wide range of different ways. You can play sports, go swimming, ride a bike or do anything that you want. It's all about enjoying yourself. So make sure that you're enjoying what you do and doing it often enough to get results.

7. Make yourself work-It can be difficult to follow a diet and exercise plan. It can be really difficult when you just don't want to do it. So make sure that you are making time in your daily routine to follow these goals and plans. You need to make a schedule and fit dieting and exercising into that schedule. If you don't make time for it then you simply won't do it. It doesn't matter what

time of the day you decide is best for you to exercise, what matters is that you get out there and do it.

8. Take small steps-if you've never gone on a diet before you might find it difficult now. So don't jump in with both feet. Slowly test the waters and get used to everything you need to do. Add one thing after another until you're finally really into your diet and you're making progress. If you try to do too much at once you get overwhelmed and you're far more likely to just give up.

9. Reward yourself-You really don't want to exercise and diet even if you do really want to lose weight. Your body really doesn't want to lose the weight at all. So that means all of these steps are hard. You have to fight yourself nearly every step of the way. So give yourself a reward when you reach smaller goals. Whether it's getting a massage or taking a vacation. Try to avoid rewarding yourself with food since that's probably what got you into this mess in the first place. You want to only splurge when you really need to and it shouldn't have anything to do with rewarding yourself.

Chapter 12- Superfoods You Should be Eating

Eating healthy is important of course and that means you should be eating a lot of fruits and vegetables and some meats as well. But did you know that some of these foods are far better for you than others? Well these special foods are called superfoods and they have more health benefits than probably anything else you eat. The foods on this list are only a few of those superfoods but they are things you should be eating in high quantities.

Below our list of superfoods is a list of some simple recipes that use common ingredients and healthy foods to help you on your weight loss goals and plans.

Super Food	**Benefits**
Blueberries	- Phytoflavonoids - Potassium - Vitamin C - Reduces risk of heart disease - Reduces risk of cancer
Fish rich in omega 3 fatty acids (i.e. wild salmon)	- Reduces risk of heart disease - Alleviates inflammation - May help with conditions like Alzheimer's
Soy	- May help lower cholesterol if eaten regularly - High in protein
Whole grains	- High in dietary fiber - Helps lower cholesterol - Detoxifies the body - Helps in regulating blood sugar levels
Dark chocolate (80% cocoa content)	- Evidence shows that dark chocolate can actually lower blood pressure - Packed with healthy antioxidants
	- Aids proper digestion

Yogurt with live probiotic culture	- Probiotic components boosts the immune system - Probiotics have been shown to reduce the number of "sick days" by as much as 50% - Studies show that dairy products help people lose weight in the long term
Oranges	- Vitamin C - Vitamin E - Iron - Light in calories but packed with health-giving nutrients; can be eaten any time of the day
Oysters	- Packed with zinc, which protects the lungs and the immune system - May help boost male reproductive function and production of spermatozoa - Zinc also helps protect your skin, hair, and nails
Black beans	- Rich source of protein - Iron - Zinc - Biotin
Walnuts	- Polyunsaturated fats - Omega 3 fatty acids - Also rich in antioxidants - Helps protect the prostate in advanced age
Tomatoes	- Vitamin C - Helps keep the prostate free from inflammation and disease - Helps prolong the youthful appearance of the skin and hair - Helps protect the skin from the ravages of excessive sun exposure
Apples	- Dietary fiber - Vitamins - Minerals - Quercetin – a potent antioxidant that prevents cellular damage by free radicals
Broccoli sprouts	- Isothiocyanates in broccoli sprouts have been known to actively combat inflammation in tissues. Studies have also shown that isothiocyanates also have the capacity

	to trigger the process that removes cancer-causing compounds from the body.
Carrots	- Beta carotene - Antioxidants - Good for the skin, too!
Olive oil	- A good source of monounsaturated fats - A better choice when cooking or making salads - Also contains polyphenols
Eggs	- Eating eggs may help aid weight loss by prolonging the feeling of satiety throughout the day - A wonderful source of fat and protein (which are both important for body functions)
Nuts	- Dietary fiber - Antioxidants - High protein content - May help lower cholesterol levels - Contains stenols - Naturally adds flavor and texture to dishes and even pureed meals
Kiwis	- Minerals - Vitamin C - Vitamin A - Vitamin E - Potassium - High in dietary fiber
Quinoa	- High protein content - High in dietary fiber - Zinc - Tocopherol - Selenium - May help ward off heart problems in the future - One of the best grains around
Broccoli	- Vitamin A - Vitamin C - Vitamin K
Sweet potatoes	- Vitamin A - Vitamin C - Potassium

	- Dietary fiber
Cabbage	- Dietary fiber - Studies show that cabbages help fight off cancer; several studies confirm that eating lots of cabbage can slash the risk of colon cancer by as much as 66% - Immunity booster - Helps purify the blood - Contains anthocyanins (potent antioxidants)
Garlic	- Garlic naturally lowers cholesterol - May help prevent cancer because of its potent antioxidant properties - Helps detoxify the body - May help remove heavy metals from the body
Mushrooms	- Immunity-boosting wonder food - Fights high blood pressure - Lowers cholesterol - Fights off viral infections - Fights off bacterial infections - Compounds in mushrooms have been shown to have the ability to shrink tumors
Flaxseeds	- Contains alpha-linoleic acid, which counters inflammation in body tissues - Healthy fatty acids - A good source of protein
Pomegranates	- The juice from the pomegranate fruit has been shown to combat the plaque build-up which causes stroke and heart attacks - May help slow down aging - May help prevent different types of cancer
Spinach	- Potassium - Magnesium - Vitamins - Dietary fiber

Chapter 13- Quick and Easy Baby Food Recipes

Recipe # 1

- 4 ounces sliced chicken breast

- Salt

- Pepper

- 2 tbsp. of butter

- 2 tbsp. of flour

- 4 ounces of fresh milk

- 32 ounces of peas

1. Warm the butter on a pan for sixty seconds.

2. Add the fresh milk and slowly stir.

3. Add the other ingredients and stir until the sauce thickens.

Recipe # 2

- 1 butternut squash

1. Bake the butternut squash for sixty minutes

2. If you don't want to bake the squash, you can just peel it and boil the chunks of butternut squash until the meat of the veggie becomes soft.

3. Scoop out the squash and puree

4. Add as much or as little water as needed so the food comes out with a desirable consistency

Recipe # 3

- 2 ounces of applesauce

- 8 ounces of cooked brown rice or white rice

- 1 butternut squash

1. Bake or boil the butternut squash until the meat of the veggie is cooked and soft.

2. Puree the butternut squash until you get the desired consistency.

3. When the butternut squash has attained the consistency that you like, puree the rice and the applesauce. Combine the applesauce, rice and butternut squash.

Recipe # 4

- 3 Macintosh apples

- Cinnamon (to taste)

- Acorn squash

1. Bake or boil the acorn squash until cooked and soft.

2. Scoop out the meat of the acorn squash and puree. Set aside.

3. Wash, peel, and slice the Macintosh apples. Puree.

4. Combine the pureed acorn squash and the pureed Macintosh apples. Add cinnamon to your liking.

Recipe # 5

- 1 squash or 1 medium sized pumpkin

- 2 ounces of water

- 1 ounce of rice (brown or white)

- 4 ounces of yogurt with live culture

1. Bake or boil the squash or pumpkin.

2. Scoop out the meat of the squash/pumpkin and puree. Add the water to thin out the consistency of the pureed vegetable.

3. Add the rice and yogurt last.

Recipe # 6

- 1 butternut squash

- Nutmeg (to taste)

- Ginger (to taste)

- Cinnamon (to taste)

- 4 ounces of raisins

- 2 tbsp. of applesauce

1. Bake or boil the butternut squash. If you want to bake it, you need to cook it in the oven for at least forty minutes until the vegetable becomes a little curled. You must then scoop out the meat and puree it.

2. After pureeing the squash, add the ginger, cinnamon, applesauce, nutmeg and raisins to the concoction.

Recipe # 7

- Butternut squash

- 1 pound of sweet potatoes

- 4 ounces of cream

- 2 tablespoons of olive oil

- 2 ounces of chives, chopped finely

1. Peel and slice the butternut squash and sweet potatoes. Add these veggies to a pan with some water and cook until tender. This usually takes around 40 minutes to complete.

2. Remove the water from the pan and add four ounces of cream.

3. Add the olive oil and chives to the concoction and puree.

Recipe # 8

- 1 banana

- 1 avocado

1. Peel and slice the avocado. Remove the put and set aside.

2. Slice the banana and put in a blender. Add the avocado slices as well.

3. Puree. Add water to modify the consistency of the pureed meal.

Recipe # 9

- 4 avocados

- 4 bananas

- 4 pears

- 8 ounces of yogurt with live culture

1. Begin by peeling and slicing the avocados in half. Remove the pits and slice the meat of the avocado into chunks.

2. Slice the bananas and set aside.

3. Steam the pears until the fruit become tender and moist.

4. Peel the pears and combine all of the ingredients in a blender.

5. Puree until the desired consistency is achieved.

Recipe # 10

- 8 ounces of fresh mango chunks

- 1 avocado

1. Peel the avocado and remove the pit. Slice the fruit into chunks.

2. Combine the mango chunks and the avocado chunks in a blender and puree.

3. Feel free to add water to thin out the concoction.

Printed in Great Britain
by Amazon